The

Entrepreneurial

Outline

Essential Strategies and
Insights for Aspiring Entrepreneurs

GARRETT FOX

Copyright © 2024 by Garrett Fox

All Rights Reserved.

No part of this book may be reproduced or transmitted in any form or by any means, electronic, or mechanical, including photocopying, recording, or by any information storage and retrieval system, without the permission of the author, except were permitted by law.

Table of Contents

Preface 1
1. The Power of an Entrepreneur Mindset 5
2. What They Don't Teach You in School 20
3. The Power of Surrounding Yourself with Like-Minded People 30
4. The Power Of Self-Investing 40
5. The Power of Knowing Your Value 54
6. The Benefit of Adding Value to Others 66
7. The Power of Being Skeptical 78
8. Don't Wait for the Right Time, NOW is the Time 87
Bio 99

Preface

My name is Garrett Fox and I have spent almost two decades now being an entrepreneur. From working in a eye doctors office at 16 and then moving states and working at another eye doctor's office and them literally creating a position that never existed on the spot and hiring me, to then managing in a music store and becoming the number one sales associate in the country, From playing drums for over 20 years getting my own signature on my drumsticks, to teching drums, working and being on the biggest stages for some of the biggest artist in music history.

From adding real estate to my resume, to becoming an award-winning agent.

I've traveled all across the country doing what I love, helping people, and achieving dreams.

I have influenced the lives of Bankers, Lawyers, Insurance Agents, Actors, Producers, Models, CEOs, other Realtors, tons of Fundraisers, and the list just keeps going.

Now why is that important?

That should be very important to you as a reader.

You want to know the person writing this book isn't just a someone who hasn't experienced anything, but I've experience successes and failures and then learning from those to gain more successes. That I am a person who has navigated through the "real world".

My success has come from a lot of what you are going to read in this book.

In this book we are going to break down the things that I have experienced, and the things that HAVE and HAVE NOT worked for me.

You may find this book very direct, you may ridicule and you may even want to throw this book out, but I ensure you it works.

As now that others people's life have changed for the better, so can yours.

In this book we are going to break down the basic steps that you should do mentally physically and spiritually to be on the path to success.

My goal is for you to learn this book through reading, listening, memorizing, role playing, implementing, and then hopefully teaching to the real world.

The goal of this book is that you the readers can take this and be a master at these basic necessary things one needs implemented to be on the path of success.

The goal is that at the end of this book you look back and reflect and see how much our mental capacity could really allow us to grow. That if you take risks you will succeed. Think outside the box.

I encourage you to read this and listen to it.

If you are listening to this I, go get the book.

If you are reading this, go get the audio version.

Read the book and listen to the audio a few times, go back and read the book and listen to the audio over again. And then make sure your friends and family get a copy and read this book so their lives can be changed as well.

I truly believe these basic necessities are that effective.

If you find yourself highlighting or underlining with a pen or pencil words or phrases in this book then you are on the right track.

If you want to have abundance in your life, implement these necessities into your life.

There is lots of information you can try to find that can be very complicated, the information you are about to read in this book is a guideline to some of most basic fundamentals you absolutely need.

If you implement these basic necessities, you can ensure that that your peers and people around you will start to look at you different and look at you as a leader someone who has ridden the ride been through the tough times and rose above.

This book is not for everyone. I say that loud and clear.

If you are "OK" with being "average", if you are a person who says I only need "just enough",

This book may not be for you. I am just saying.

It is our duty to want to have a better life, and want to live in abundance, to not just provide for our own family and livelihood, but to give back to the people that have helped us along the way. To say "thank you!" Because let's face it most of us have been there.

If you are a person that says I want to do better, and I want to be better.

Then this book is EXACTLY for you.

Their will be students, teachers, CEOs, business men and women, and many many more who once doubted themselves implement these basic necessities. Who once had limiting beliefs and now are making their dreams a reality. I hope you are one of them.

I can't wait to hear your story on how this book changed your life.

1

The Power of an Entrepreneur Mindset

"Your mindset shapes your destiny; think like an entrepreneur, and the world becomes your opportunity."

An entrepreneur is someone who is constantly on the lookout for opportunities, particularly those that can lead to profit and personal growth. But beyond this simple definition, an entrepreneur is someone who seeks to improve themselves and their surroundings continuously. The entrepreneurial journey begins with the question, "How can I make a positive impact today?"

To succeed as an entrepreneur, it's essential to develop a mindset that encompasses four critical components:

A. Attitude

B. Creativity

C. Relationships

D. Organizational Skills

These four elements are the foundation of entrepreneurial success. Let's dive deeper into each of these components.

Attitude:

The first component, and arguably the most important, is your attitude. A positive attitude is non-negotiable in the world of entrepreneurship. It's not just about how you feel on a good day, but how you perceive and respond to challenges and setbacks. Your attitude shapes your actions, and your actions, in turn, shape your success.

Consider this: when you encounter a difficult situation, do you immediately see it as an obstacle, or do you view it as an opportunity for growth? The way you choose to perceive the situation will determine your response. A negative attitude leads to frustration and inaction, while a positive attitude inspires solutions and progress.

Having a positive attitude means looking for the silver lining in every situation. It's about seeing opportunities where others see problems. For example, when a business deal falls through, do you dwell on the loss, or do you focus on what you can learn from the experience and how you can pivot to create new opportunities? Successful entrepreneurs are those who can pivot with grace and keep moving forward with optimism, even in the face of adversity.

Your attitude is a reflection of your mindset. It's a choice you make every day, in every situation. To cultivate a positive attitude, you must be intentional about how you think and how you speak to yourself. Affirmations, gratitude, and a focus on solutions rather than problems are all tools you can use to develop and maintain a positive attitude.

It's also important to surround yourself with people who uplift you and contribute to a positive environment. Negativity is contagious, but so is positivity. Build a support network of like-minded individuals who encourage you to see the best in every situation and who will hold you accountable when your attitude starts to waver.

Remember, your attitude is the lens through which you view the world. It can either distort reality or bring it into sharp focus. A positive attitude, grounded in a growth mindset, will help you navigate the ups and downs of entrepreneurship with resilience and grace.

Creativity:

Creativity is the lifeblood of entrepreneurship. It's the ability to think outside the box, to innovate, and to solve problems in new and unexpected ways. Creativity is what sets entrepreneurs apart from the crowd and drives them to pursue unique opportunities that others might overlook.

To be a successful entrepreneur, you must cultivate creativity in every aspect of your life and work. Creativity isn't just about artistic expression; it's about finding new solutions to old problems, developing innovative products or services, and continually pushing the boundaries of what's possible.

Consider the great entrepreneurs of our time—Steve Jobs, Elon Musk, Oprah Winfrey—they are all known for their creative thinking and their ability to see possibilities where others see limitations. They are not just creators; they are innovators, constantly thinking several steps ahead, much like a master chess player who anticipates the moves of their opponent before they happen.

Creativity also requires a willingness to embrace change and to adapt when things don't go as planned. In the world of entrepreneurship, flexibility is key. You must be able to pivot when necessary and find new paths to achieve your goals. This often means thinking outside the box and coming up with creative solutions to challenges that arise.

But creativity doesn't just happen on its own; it's something that needs to be nurtured and developed. One way to do this is by exposing yourself to new experiences and ideas. Travel, read widely, attend conferences, and engage in activities that challenge your thinking. The more you expose yourself to different perspectives, the more creative you'll become.

Another important aspect of creativity is the ability to finish what you start. It's easy to have a great idea, but it takes creativity and perseverance to bring that idea to fruition. Successful entrepreneurs are finishers; they follow through on their ideas and see them through to the end, even when the going gets tough.

Creativity also requires you to think long-term. It's not just about solving the problems of today; it's about anticipating the challenges of tomorrow and coming up with solutions before they become issues. This forward-thinking approach is what separates the successful entrepreneur from the rest.

Finally, remember that creativity isn't just about innovation; it's also about problem-solving. When faced with a challenge, ask yourself, "How can I solve this in a new and better way?" This mindset will help you stay ahead of the curve and keep your business moving forward.

Relationships:

The third key component of the entrepreneurial mindset is relationships. As the saying goes, **"It's not about who you know, but who knows you."** In entrepreneurship, relationships are everything. They are the foundation upon which businesses are built and the fuel that drives growth and success.

Building and maintaining strong relationships is essential for any entrepreneur. This means not only networking and meeting new people but also nurturing the relationships you already have. Successful entrepreneurs understand the value of relationships and invest time and energy into building a network of supporters, collaborators, and mentors.

One of the most important aspects of building relationships is being genuine. People can tell when you're being inauthentic, and nothing turns people off faster than a lack of sincerity. When you approach relationships with authenticity and a genuine desire to connect with others, you'll find that people are more willing to help you and support your endeavors.

Another key to building strong relationships is to be a giver, not just a taker. Successful relationships are built on mutual respect and reciprocity. Be willing to help others without expecting anything in return, and you'll find that people are more likely to want to help you when you need it. This is what I call "coming from contribution," a concept we'll dive deeper into in Chapter 6.

Networking is a critical part of relationship-building. Whether it's attending seminars, conferences, or setting up coffee meetings with other professionals, getting out and meeting people is essential for your success. Networking isn't just about collecting business cards; it's about building meaningful connections that can help you grow your business and achieve your goals.

Think of networking like planting seeds. Each time you meet someone new, you're planting a seed that has the potential to grow into a valuable relationship. Some of these seeds will blossom into strong, long-lasting relationships, while others may not take root. But the more seeds you plant, the greater your chances of success.

It's also important to be intentional about the relationships you build. Surround yourself with people who inspire you, challenge you, and push you to be your best. These are the relationships that will help you grow as an entrepreneur and achieve your goals.

Remember, relationships are a two-way street. You can't expect others to invest in you if you're not willing to invest in them. Take the time to nurture your relationships, stay in touch, and offer support whenever you can. The more you give, the more you'll receive in return.

Organization:

The final key component of the entrepreneurial mindset is organization. In the fast-paced world of entrepreneurship, staying organized is essential for success. It's not enough to have great ideas and strong relationships; you also need the systems and processes in place to execute your plans effectively.

Many successful entrepreneurs will tell you that organization is the key to their success. This includes having a reliable follow-up system, using a calendar to manage your time, and having a clear plan for your day, week, and month. Without organization, even the best ideas can fall by the wayside.

One of the most important aspects of organization is the ability to prioritize. As an entrepreneur, you'll have a million things on your plate at any given time. It's crucial to know which tasks are most important and to focus your time and energy on those tasks. This is where a good planning system comes in handy.

For example, at the start of each week, take some time to plan out your goals and tasks for the week. Break down your goals into actionable steps and prioritize them based on their importance. This will help you stay focused and ensure that you're making progress on the things that matter most.

Another important aspect of organization is the ability to keep track of important information. Whether it's client details, project deadlines, or financial records, having a system in place to manage your information is critical. This could be as simple as using a digital note-taking app, a project management tool, or even just a well-organized filing system.

Labeling and categorizing your information can also help you stay organized. Successful entrepreneurs often have systems in place for everything, from their email folders to their desktop files to their calendar. These systems help them stay on top of their responsibilities and ensure that nothing falls through the cracks.

It's also important to have a backup plan. No matter how organized you are, things can go wrong. Whether it's losing a notebook or having your computer crash, having a backup system in place can save you a lot of stress and headaches. This could mean regularly backing up your files to the cloud, keeping important documents in multiple locations, or having a contingency plan for unexpected events.

In addition to these practical tips, organization also involves having a clear vision and strategy for your business. This means knowing where you want to go and having a plan for how you're going to get there. Without a clear direction, it's easy to get lost in the day-to-day grind and lose sight of your long-term goals.

Remember, organization is about creating order out of chaos. It's about having a system in place that allows you to focus on what's important and ensures that you're always moving forward. The more organized you are, the more efficient and effective you'll be as an entrepreneur.

As you embark on your entrepreneurial journey, remember that you don't have to do it all on your own. Even the most successful entrepreneurs need help from time to time. It's important to recognize your strengths and weaknesses and to seek help in the areas where you need it.

Whether it's hiring a virtual assistant, outsourcing tasks, or seeking advice from a mentor, don't be afraid to ask for help. No one achieves success alone, and building a strong support network is essential for your success.

Surround yourself with winners—people who inspire you, challenge you, and push you to be your best.

These are the people who will help you stay motivated, keep you accountable, and support you on your journey.

Never stop learning. The world of entrepreneurship is constantly evolving, and staying ahead of the curve requires continuous education. Whether it's reading books, listening to podcasts, attending conferences, or taking online courses, make learning a priority. The more knowledge you have, the better equipped you'll be to navigate the challenges and opportunities that come your way.

One of the most powerful tools you have as an entrepreneur is your mind. Developing an entrepreneurial mindset requires intentionality and effort, but the rewards are well worth it. As Bruce Lee famously said, "Be like water." Water is adaptable, powerful, and able to flow around obstacles with ease. In the same way, you must be adaptable, resilient, and ready to pivot when necessary.

The entrepreneurial mindset is not something you're born with; it's something you develop over time. With the right mindset, anything is possible. Success in entrepreneurship requires a strong mental attitude, a willingness to take risks, and the perseverance to keep going, even when the going gets tough.

Accountability and Discipline:

Two of the most critical qualities for success in entrepreneurship are accountability and discipline. Without these, even the best ideas and intentions can fall short.

Accountability means taking ownership of your actions, your decisions, and your results. It's about being responsible for your commitments to yourself and others. When you hold yourself accountable, you're more likely to follow through on your goals and stay on track.

One way to build accountability is to set clear, specific goals and to regularly review your progress. Whether it's daily, weekly, or monthly, taking the time to check in on your goals will help you stay focused and motivated. If you find that you're not making the progress you'd like, ask yourself why and what you can do to get back on track.

Another way to build accountability is to share your goals with others. This could be a mentor, a business partner, or even just a friend. When you share your goals with someone else, you're more likely to stick to them because you don't want to let that person down. Plus, having someone to hold you accountable can be a powerful motivator.

Discipline, on the other hand, is about having the willpower to make the right choices, even when it's difficult. It's about sticking to your plans, following through on your commitments, and staying focused on your long-term goals.

Discipline is what keeps you going when motivation wanes. It's what gets you out of bed in the morning, even when you'd rather hit the snooze button. It's what helps you stay focused on your work, even when distractions are all around you.

Building discipline requires practice and consistency. Start by setting small, achievable goals and gradually increase the difficulty as you build your discipline muscles. The more you practice discipline, the easier it will become.

Remember, accountability and discipline go hand in hand. When you hold yourself accountable, you're more likely to be disciplined in your actions. And when you're disciplined, you're more likely to achieve your goals and stay on track.

Creative Avoidance:

One of the biggest obstacles to success in entrepreneurship is creative avoidance. This is when you find ways to avoid the tasks you know you need to do, often by doing something that feels productive but isn't actually moving you closer to your goals.

Creative avoidance can take many forms. It could be spending hours organizing your workspace instead of making sales calls, endlessly tweaking your website instead of launching it, or getting caught up in busywork instead of focusing on your most important tasks.

The key to overcoming creative avoidance is to be aware of it and to take action to address it. One way to do this is to identify your most important tasks—the tasks that will have the biggest impact on your business—and to focus on those tasks first.

Another way to overcome creative avoidance is to break down large, daunting tasks into smaller, more manageable steps. When a task feels overwhelming, it's easy to procrastinate. But when you break it down into smaller steps, it becomes more manageable and less intimidating.

It's also important to set boundaries for yourself. This could mean setting specific times for checking email, limiting the amount of time you spend on social media, or blocking out time on your calendar for focused work. The more you can minimize distractions and stay focused on your most important tasks, the more productive you'll be.

Remember, the goal is progress, not perfection. It's better to take imperfect action than to do nothing at all. Don't let the fear of making mistakes or the desire for perfection hold you back. Take action, learn from your mistakes, and keep moving forward.

Learning from Others' Mistakes:

One of the best ways to accelerate your success as an entrepreneur is to learn from others' mistakes, not just your own. While making mistakes is a natural part of the learning process, you can save yourself a lot of time and headaches by learning from the experiences of others.

This could mean reading books and articles by successful entrepreneurs, listening to podcasts and interviews, or seeking advice from mentors and peers. The more you learn from others' experiences, the better equipped you'll be to navigate the challenges and opportunities that come your way.

One way to do this is to seek out stories of failure as well as success. It's easy to focus on the success stories, but the failures often contain the most valuable lessons. By understanding what went wrong and how others overcame their challenges, you can avoid making the same mistakes and increase your chances of success.

Another way to learn from others' mistakes is to seek feedback on your own work. Whether it's from a mentor, a peer, or a customer, getting feedback can help you identify potential issues before they become problems. Be open to constructive criticism and use it to improve your work and grow as an entrepreneur.

Remember, success in entrepreneurship is not just about avoiding mistakes; it's about learning from them and using that knowledge to grow and improve. The more you learn from others' experiences, the faster you'll be able to achieve your own success.

The Power of Visualization:

Visualization is a powerful tool for success in entrepreneurship. It's about creating a mental image of your goals and the steps you need to take to achieve them. When you visualize your success, you're more likely to stay focused, motivated, and committed to your goals.

Visualization is not just about imagining the end result; it's about visualizing the entire process. This includes the challenges you'll face, the obstacles you'll overcome, and the actions you'll take to achieve your goals. By visualizing the process, you can prepare yourself mentally for the journey ahead and increase your chances of success.

One way to practice visualization is to set aside time each day to focus on your goals and imagine yourself achieving them. This could be in the morning, before you start your day, or in the evening, before you go to bed. The key is to make visualization a regular part of your routine.

Another way to practice visualization is to create a vision board. This is a physical representation of your goals and dreams, using images, quotes, and other visual elements. By keeping your vision board in a place where you'll see it every day, you'll be reminded of your goals and stay motivated to achieve them.

Remember, visualization is a tool to help you stay focused and motivated. It's not a substitute for hard work and action, but it can be a powerful complement to your efforts. The more you visualize your success, the more likely you are to achieve it.

Conclusion:

The entrepreneurial mindset is the foundation of success in business and in life. It's about adopting the habits, attitudes, and actions of successful people and using them to achieve your own goals.

The battle in your mind is the most important one you'll face. Your thoughts shape your actions, and your actions shape your results. By cultivating a positive attitude, staying creative, building strong relationships, and staying organized, you can set yourself up for success.

Success in entrepreneurship is not about quick wins; it's about consistent growth and multiple income streams. It's about having the discipline and accountability to stay on track and the willingness to learn from your mistakes and the mistakes of others.

Starting young with these principles gives you a head start in the entrepreneurial journey. Whether it's working at a young age or selling candy bars, early experiences shape your mindset. Teach children about money, finance, and the difference between assets and liabilities. You might be surprised at what they can grasp.

Visualize your success. The mind is your greatest tool—train it well, and it will lead you to success.

In the end, the entrepreneurial journey is about more than just building a business; it's about building a life that reflects your values, your passions, and your vision for the future. It's about making a positive impact on the world and leaving a legacy that will inspire others to do the same.

So as you embark on your entrepreneurial journey, remember: **"Change your mindset, change your actions, change your life."**

With the right mindset, anything is possible.

2

What They Don't Teach You in School

"Success isn't found in textbooks but in the trials, failures, and relentless pursuit of your goals."

When we think about what's traditionally taught in school, the first things that come to mind are reading, writing, and arithmetic—the foundational pillars of education that have been drilled into us from a young age. But as we grow older, we realize that there are many crucial lessons about life and success that aren't covered in textbooks or taught in classrooms. These are the lessons that often separate those who thrive in the entrepreneurial world from those who struggle to find their footing.

The Illusion of Security: Breaking the Mold

From a young age, we're taught that life follows a predictable, linear path: do well in school, go to college, get a degree, secure a stable job, work hard, and eventually retire with enough savings to live comfortably. This blueprint is ingrained into us as the key to a successful and secure life. But let's take a step back and question this narrative—what does security really mean in today's fast-paced, ever-changing world?

In reality, the idea of security that we cling to is often an illusion. A steady paycheck and a stable job might feel safe, but how secure are they truly? In an era where industries are being disrupted overnight by technological advancements and global markets are increasingly volatile, the concept of job security is no longer as reliable as it once was. Companies can downsize without warning, entire professions can become obsolete, and economic recessions can wipe out years of hard work in a matter of months.

What they don't teach you in school is that real security doesn't come from adhering to this outdated blueprint. True financial stability and security are achieved through diversification—by creating multiple streams of income that aren't tied to a single employer, industry, or even economy. This means investing in a variety of assets, such as stocks, real estate, and businesses, and continually seeking out new opportunities to grow your wealth. By diversifying your income, you create a financial safety net that can withstand the unpredictable tides of the economy. When one stream of income dries up, others can keep you afloat, providing a level of security that a traditional job could never offer.

The Power of Networking: Building a Strong Foundation

In school, the focus is often on individual achievement—your grades, your test scores, your ability to succeed on your own. While these metrics are important in an academic setting, they don't fully prepare you for the realities of the business world, where relationships and connections are often just as important, if not more so, than individual accomplishments.

The real world operates on a different set of rules. The most successful entrepreneurs understand that building and maintaining strong relationships is key to opening doors, creating opportunities, and ultimately achieving success. It's not always about being the smartest or the most talented person in the room; often, it's about knowing the right people—those who can offer guidance, provide resources, or open up new avenues for growth.

Yet, traditional education rarely teaches us the importance of networking, nor does it equip us with the skills needed to build meaningful, mutually beneficial relationships. Networking isn't about collecting business cards or racking up connections on LinkedIn. It's about cultivating a community of people who support each other's growth, who offer value without expecting anything in return, and who understand that success is often a collaborative effort.

To truly excel in the entrepreneurial world, you need to master the art of networking. This means going beyond superficial interactions and building genuine relationships based on trust, respect, and mutual benefit. It means understanding the needs and goals of others and finding ways to help them achieve those goals, knowing that, in turn, they will be more likely to help you achieve yours. The power of networking lies in the strength of your relationships, and this is a lesson that's often neglected in formal education but is absolutely critical to long-term success.

The Value of Failure: Embracing Setbacks

Failure is often portrayed as the enemy in traditional education. We're taught to avoid it at all costs, to fear it, and to view it as a sign of weakness or incompetence. A bad grade, a failed project, or a low score on a standardized test is something to be ashamed of, something that could potentially derail our future success. But this mindset is not only limiting—it's also fundamentally flawed.

In the entrepreneurial world, failure is not just inevitable; it's necessary. Every successful entrepreneur has a long list of failures under their belt, and these failures are not viewed as setbacks, but as valuable learning experiences. Each failure provides crucial insights—what doesn't work, what to avoid, how to pivot—and these insights are what ultimately lead to success.

What they don't teach you in school is that failure is an essential part of the learning process. It's through failure that we gain the knowledge and experience needed to succeed. The most successful entrepreneurs are those who have failed repeatedly, learned from their mistakes, and continued to push forward with renewed determination. They understand that each failure brings them one step closer to success.

Instead of fearing failure, we should embrace it. We should view it as a stepping stone on the path to success, a necessary part of the journey that helps us grow and improve. Failure is not the opposite of success; it's a critical component of it. The more we fail, the more we learn, and the closer we get to achieving our goals.

The Importance of Self-Education: Taking Control of Your Learning

The traditional education system is designed to provide a broad foundation of knowledge, covering a wide range of subjects and disciplines. But this broad approach often comes at the expense of depth, and many of the most important lessons about life and success are left out of the curriculum. What they don't teach you in school is that the most valuable education often happens outside the classroom.

Self-education—taking the initiative to learn on your own—is a critical skill that isn't taught in school. It's the key to staying relevant in a rapidly changing world, where the ability to adapt and learn new skills is more important than ever. Successful entrepreneurs understand this. They are lifelong learners who constantly seek out new knowledge, whether it's through books, seminars, podcasts, or conversations with mentors. They know that the world is evolving, and to stay ahead, they must evolve too.

While a formal education can provide a solid foundation, it's the knowledge you seek out on your own that will set you apart. In a world where information is more accessible than ever, those who continue to learn and adapt are the ones who will thrive. Your formal education might end with graduation, but your real education—self-education—should never stop.

The Myth of Work-Life Balance: Redefining Success

We often hear about the importance of work-life balance, the idea that we should strive to evenly divide our time and energy between our professional and personal lives. But the reality, especially for entrepreneurs, is far more complex. The idea of balance often implies that work and life are two opposing forces that must be carefully managed, but this black-and-white thinking doesn't align with the messy, unpredictable nature of real life.

What they don't teach you in school is that the pursuit of work-life balance is more about integration than balance. When you're building something meaningful, whether it's a business, a creative project, or a career, it often requires intense focus and energy. During these times, work may take priority, and that's okay. The key is to find fulfillment in both your work and personal life, even if they aren't always perfectly balanced.

Sometimes, work will demand more of your time, and other times, personal commitments will. Rather than striving for a perfect 50/50 split, aim to integrate your work and personal life in a way that feels authentic and sustainable to you. Understand that at different stages of your life, the scales will tip in different directions. What matters most is that you find meaning and satisfaction in all areas, regardless of how they weigh against each other at any given moment.

The Real Cost of Success: Understanding the Trade-Offs

Success is often depicted as a glamorous destination—big houses, luxury cars, financial freedom. But what's often overlooked is the price that comes with it. School teaches us to chase traditional markers of success, like a high salary or a prestigious title, but it rarely prompts us to consider what success really means to us personally.

The cost of success isn't just financial; it can be emotional, mental, and even spiritual. What they don't teach you in school is that success isn't a one-size-fits-all concept. True success is about much more than material wealth. It's about living a life that's aligned with your values, passions, and purpose. It's about the freedom to choose how you spend your time, who you spend it with, and what you focus on.

Achieving success often requires sacrifices—time away from loved ones, relentless focus, and the willingness to push through challenges that others might shy away from. It's essential to understand what you're willing to trade for your version of success and to ensure that the pursuit doesn't cost you more than it's worth. In the end, success should enhance your life, not consume it. Define success on your terms and pursue it in a way that enriches your life rather than depletes it.

The Entrepreneurial Mindset: Shifting Your Perspective

As we discussed in the previous chapter, the entrepreneurial mindset is crucial to achieving success.

But this mindset doesn't just happen overnight—it requires a fundamental shift in the way you think about money, success, and life in general. What they don't teach you in school is that your mindset is one of the most powerful tools you have at your disposal.

The traditional education system often instills a scarcity mindset—the belief that resources are limited, that you must compete with others to get your share, and that there's only so much success to go around. But the entrepreneurial mindset is rooted in abundance—the belief that there's more than enough success, wealth, and opportunity for everyone. This shift in perspective can be life-changing.

Instead of viewing others as competitors, successful entrepreneurs see them as potential collaborators. They understand that by working together, everyone can achieve more. They embrace the idea of creating value, knowing that the more value they create for others, the more value they will receive in return.

The entrepreneurial mindset also involves a willingness to take risks, to step outside your comfort zone, and to embrace uncertainty. It's about being proactive rather than reactive, about taking control of your destiny rather than letting life happen to you. This mindset is not something that's taught in school, but it's absolutely essential for achieving long-term success.

The Long Game: Patience and Persistence

One of the most important lessons that school often fails to teach is the value of patience and persistence. In a world where instant gratification is the norm, the idea of working hard for something over a long period of time can seem foreign. But the truth is, real success rarely happens overnight.

Building a successful business, career, or life takes time. It requires consistent effort, dedication, and a willingness to keep going even when the going gets tough. What they don't teach you in school is that success is a marathon, not a sprint. It's about playing the long game—focusing on the big picture, setting long-term goals, and being willing to put in the work day after day, year after year.

Patience and persistence are the keys to overcoming obstacles and achieving your goals. There will be times when progress seems slow, when setbacks occur, and when it feels like you're not getting anywhere. But it's during these times that your perseverance will be tested. Those who succeed are the ones who keep going, who continue to push forward even when the odds are stacked against them.

Conclusion: Beyond the Classroom

The lessons we've explored in this chapter highlight the significant gap between what's taught in traditional education and the realities of the entrepreneurial journey. Schools equip us with basic knowledge, but they often fall short in preparing us for the complexities of building a successful, fulfilling life. The true education—the one that will shape your future—begins when you step beyond the classroom walls.

As you move forward in this book, keep these lessons in mind. The security, networking, resilience, self-education, balance, and definitions of success we've discussed are foundational pillars of entrepreneurship. They are the tools you'll need to navigate the challenges and seize the opportunities that come your way.

Remember, the world doesn't reward those who simply follow the rules—it rewards those who understand the rules, question them, and then create their own. Your education is in your hands now. Use it to build a life that not only meets your needs but fulfills your deepest aspirations. The journey ahead won't always be easy, but it will be worth it, and the knowledge you gain along the way will be your greatest asset.

3

The Power of Surrounding Yourself with Like-Minded People

"Success breeds success; align yourself with those who share your vision, and watch your dreams take flight."

The Foundation of Success: Your Circle of Influence

There's an old and powerful proverb that states, **"Show me your friends, and I will tell you your future."** It's a simple yet profound truth that underscores the importance of the people you choose to surround yourself with. The reality is that your environment significantly shapes who you are, how you think, and ultimately, the outcomes you achieve in life. This is especially true in the world of entrepreneurship, where your success is closely tied to your ability to navigate challenges, stay motivated, and continuously evolve.

If you find yourself as the most successful, knowledgeable, or ambitious person in your current group of friends, it might be time to reassess your circle. Growth, both personal and professional, often requires that we step outside of our comfort zones and immerse ourselves in environments that challenge us to reach new heights. This might mean seeking out new friends, mentors, and colleagues who are operating at a higher level and can inspire you to elevate your game.

The Influence of Your Inner Circle

Your inner circle—the people you spend the most time with—can either propel you toward success or hold you back. If your friends don't celebrate your wins, or worse, if they seem indifferent or even resentful of your achievements, then you're in the wrong company. True friends should not only be your biggest cheerleaders but also your most honest critics, pushing you to achieve more and holding you accountable to your goals.

The energy you absorb from those around you is crucial. Confidence, like many other traits, is contagious. When you surround yourself with winners—people who are confident, driven, and successful—you begin to adopt a similar mindset. You start to see opportunities where others see obstacles, and you become more resilient in the face of challenges. On the other hand, if you're spending your time with people who lack ambition, who are content with mediocrity, or who prefer to spend their days playing video games and their nights at the bar, it's only a matter of time before their habits start to rub off on you. This doesn't mean you need to cut ties with everyone who doesn't share your level of ambition, but it does mean that you need to be mindful of how much time and energy you're investing in those relationships.

The Power of Association: Elevating Your Average

There's a popular saying that you are the average of the five people you spend the most time with. This concept, while seemingly simplistic, holds a lot of truth. If your closest friends are constantly partying, with no real direction or drive in life, then you're likely to adopt similar habits and attitudes. Conversely, if your inner circle consists of individuals who are ambitious, goal-oriented, and relentless in their pursuit of success, you're much more likely to embody those traits yourself.

The company you keep has a profound impact on your mindset, your habits, and ultimately, your success. To truly thrive, you need to surround yourself with people who vibrate on the same wavelength as you—individuals who share your passion for growth and who are committed to achieving greatness. These are the people who will inspire you to push beyond your limits, who will challenge you to think bigger, and who will support you when the going gets tough.

The Anatomy of a Winning Circle

Building a network of like-minded individuals isn't something that happens by chance. It requires deliberate action and a clear understanding of what you want to achieve. Here's a step-by-step process that has worked for me, and that I believe can work for you if you're committed to putting in the necessary effort.

Step One: Define Your Ideal Network

The first step in building a successful network is to clearly define the type of people you want to have in your life. This requires introspection and honesty. Ask yourself: What qualities do these people possess? What level of success have they achieved? What values do they uphold? Are they positive, motivated, and driven, or are they complacent and content with mediocrity?

It's important to be as specific as possible when defining your ideal network. Consider the attributes that matter most to you—whether it's integrity, ambition, creativity, or resilience. By having a clear vision of the type of individuals you want to attract, you'll be better equipped to identify where these people might be found and how you can align your actions to meet them.

But it's not just about professional success. You also want to surround yourself with people who are kind, generous, and supportive. The right network will not only help you achieve your professional goals but will also enrich your life on a personal level. These are the people who will be there to celebrate your successes, offer advice when you need it, and provide support when you face challenges.

Step Two: Become a Magnet for Success

Once you've defined the type of people you want in your life, the next step is to become the type of person they would want to associate with. This means focusing on your own growth and development so that you can bring value to those around you.

Successful people are naturally drawn to others who share their drive, discipline, and commitment to excellence. If you're lazy, unmotivated, or lack discipline, it's unlikely that someone who is successful will want to spend time with you. So, focus on putting yourself in a position to be successful. This might involve developing new skills, adopting healthier habits, or setting higher standards for yourself.

One of the most important things you can do is to simply show up—whether it's at networking events, industry conferences, or even online communities. It's hard to compete with the elite if you're not even at the starting line. By showing up, you're signaling to others that you're serious about your goals and that you're ready to put in the work necessary to achieve them.

Another key aspect of becoming a magnet for success is to consistently demonstrate value. This could be through sharing your knowledge and expertise, offering help or support to others, or simply being someone who others enjoy being around. When you bring value to others, they'll be more likely to want to spend time with you and to introduce you to other successful individuals in their network.

Step Three: Take Action

Knowing what to do is only half the battle. The real challenge lies in taking action. Once you've identified the steps you need to take, it's time to execute. Don't just think about it—do it. This is where many people fall short. They have the best of intentions, but they never follow through. To be successful, you need to be willing to put in the work day in and day out.

Put yourself in environments that foster growth and success. Attend conferences, join seminars, and seek out coaching from those who have already walked the path you're on. The more you immerse yourself in these environments, the more you'll learn, grow, and connect with others who share your ambitions.

Taking action also means being proactive in seeking out opportunities to expand your network. This might involve reaching out to potential mentors, attending industry events, or even joining online communities where you can connect with like-minded individuals. The more you put yourself out there, the more opportunities you'll have to meet people who can help you achieve your goals.

The Role of Mentorship in Your Network

One of the most valuable relationships you can develop within your network is that of a mentor. A mentor is someone who has already achieved what you're striving for and can offer guidance, advice, and support as you navigate your own path to success.

Finding the right mentor can be a game-changer in your entrepreneurial journey. A good mentor will not only provide you with the benefit of their experience but will also challenge you to think differently, push you out of your comfort zone, and hold you accountable to your goals. They can offer insights into potential pitfalls, help you navigate challenges, and provide valuable feedback that can accelerate your growth.

To find a mentor, start by identifying individuals in your industry or field who you admire and respect. Reach out to them, express your admiration for their work, and ask if they would be willing to meet with you. Be clear about what you hope to gain from the relationship and how you can provide value in return. Remember, mentorship is a two-way street. While your mentor will provide you with guidance and support, you should also be prepared to offer something in return, whether it's your time, skills, or even just your willingness to listen and learn.

The Benefits of Networking: Expanding Your Horizons

Networking is about more than just making connections—it's about expanding your horizons, learning from others, and opening yourself up to new opportunities. Early in my journey, I attended Coach Michael Burt's "Monster Nation" conference. It was a transformative experience that opened my eyes to the power of networking.

At the conference, I met countless successful individuals who shared my level of motivation and drive. These were people who were not just talking about success but living it. The relationships I built there led to coffee meetings, business partnerships, and a wealth of knowledge that I wouldn't have gained otherwise.

By surrounding myself with others who had already achieved what I was striving for, I was able to learn from their experiences—what worked, what didn't, and how they overcame obstacles along the way. I walked away from that conference not only with new connections but also with a renewed sense of purpose and a clearer vision of what I wanted to achieve.

Networking also provides you with the opportunity to learn from others' mistakes and successes. Every entrepreneur has their own unique journey, and by connecting with others, you can gain valuable insights that can help you avoid common pitfalls and accelerate your own success.

The Ripple Effect: How Your Network Impacts Your Life

The people you surround yourself with don't just influence your professional success—they also have a profound impact on your personal life. Your network can provide you with emotional support, encouragement, and a sense of community.

They can help you stay grounded during challenging times and celebrate your successes when you achieve your goals.

In addition to the direct benefits of networking, there's also a ripple effect that occurs when you surround yourself with like-minded individuals. When you're part of a network of successful, motivated people, you're more likely to stay focused on your goals, to push yourself to achieve more, and to hold yourself to a higher standard. This, in turn, can lead to greater success in all areas of your life.

Your network also has the power to open doors to new opportunities that you might not have otherwise had access to. Whether it's a job opportunity, a business partnership, or an investment deal, the right connections can make all the difference. This is why it's so important to be intentional about the people you surround yourself with and to continuously seek out opportunities to expand your network.

Creating a Culture of Growth: The Value of Accountability

One of the key benefits of surrounding yourself with like-minded individuals is the accountability that comes with it. When you're part of a group of driven, goal-oriented people, there's a natural tendency to hold each other accountable. This can be incredibly valuable in helping you stay on track with your goals and pushing you to achieve more.

Accountability can take many forms, from regular check-ins with a mentor or accountability partner to joining a mastermind group where you can share your goals, challenges, and progress with others. The important thing is to create a culture of growth where you and those around you are constantly challenging each other to be better, do more, and reach higher.

In addition to holding each other accountable, a strong network can also provide you with valuable feedback and perspective. When you're working towards a goal, it's easy to get caught up in the day-to-day details and lose sight of the bigger picture. By sharing your progress and challenges with others, you can gain new insights, identify potential blind spots, and get the support you need to keep moving forward.

The Long-Term Impact of Your Network

The impact of your network extends far beyond your immediate goals and achievements. The relationships you build today can have a lasting impact on your life and career for years to come. As you continue to grow and evolve, so too will your network, providing you with ongoing support, opportunities, and inspiration.

One of the most important things to remember is that building a strong network is a long-term investment. It's not something that happens overnight, and it requires ongoing effort and commitment. But the rewards are well worth it. By surrounding yourself with the right people, you'll not only increase your chances of success but also create a rich, fulfilling life filled with meaningful relationships and opportunities.

Conclusion: The Path to Success Starts with Your Circle

In the end, the people you choose to surround yourself with can either propel you towards your goals or hold you back. If you're serious about achieving success, then it's crucial to be intentional about who you allow into your inner circle. Seek out those who share your vision, who are driven by the same passions, and who are committed to personal and professional growth.

The journey of entrepreneurship is challenging, but when you have the right people by your side, the path becomes clearer, the challenges more manageable, and the victories even sweeter. The steps I've outlined in this chapter are not a guaranteed formula for success, but they have worked for me and countless others. The rest is up to you. Surround yourself with the right people, take action, and watch as your life begins to transform in ways you never thought possible.

4

The Power Of Self-Investing

"Invest in yourself today, and the dividends will pay out for a lifetime."

Becoming an entrepreneur is one of the most rewarding yet challenging paths you can take. It's a journey filled with triumphs, failures, and endless learning. While many focus on business strategies, market analysis, and financial planning, one fundamental aspect often gets overlooked: the importance of investing in yourself. This chapter explores why and how you should prioritize personal development and self-investment as an entrepreneur.

Understanding the Concept of Self-Investment

Before diving into specifics, let's first understand what it means to invest in yourself. Self-investment goes beyond superficial aspects like attending workshops or obtaining certifications. It's about dedicating time, energy, and resources to your growth, well-being, and overall development. It encompasses everything from expanding your knowledge base, enhancing your skills, maintaining your physical and mental health, and fostering meaningful relationships.

Investing in yourself is the foundation upon which your business can grow and thrive. A business is often a reflection of its founder. If you are constantly evolving, learning, and improving, your business will likely follow suit. Conversely, if you neglect your personal development, your business may stagnate or, worse even, decline.

The Importance of Continuous Learning

The world of business and success is ever-changing. New technologies emerge, market trends shift, and consumer behaviors evolve. As an entrepreneur, staying ahead of these changes is crucial. This is where continuous learning comes into play.

Continuous learning is the process of constantly acquiring new knowledge and skills. It could be formal, such as pursuing higher education or certifications, or informal, like reading books like this one, attending seminars, or listening to podcasts. The goal is to stay informed and adaptable.

The Role of Formal Education

Many successful entrepreneurs advocate for the power of formal education, even if it's not in a traditional sense. Enrolling in specialized courses or obtaining certifications can provide you with a structured way of learning new concepts that are directly applicable to your business.

For instance, if you're running a tech startup, learning about the latest advancements in cybersecurity could be invaluable. If your business is in retail, a course on consumer psychology might provide insights into better marketing strategies. The key is to identify areas where you lack expertise and find educational opportunities that can fill those gaps.

Furthermore, formal education can provide you with credibility in your field. As an entrepreneur, especially in the early stages, establishing trust with customers, investors, and partners is crucial. Having a formal education or certification in your area of business can lend you that credibility and help you stand out in a competitive market. This is not always true... we will talk more about that later.

Formal education also provides an opportunity to network with peers and industry professionals. Whether you're attending a traditional university, an online course, or a professional seminar, the connections you make can be invaluable. These connections could lead to potential business partnerships, collaborations, or simply a support network of like-minded individuals who understand the challenges of entrepreneurship.

For those looking to deepen their expertise, pursuing advanced degrees or specialized certifications can be particularly beneficial. An MBA or a specialized master's degree in fields such as finance, marketing, or technology can equip you with the knowledge and skills necessary to manage complex business operations and navigate the global market. Moreover, these programs often include case studies, group projects, and simulations that mirror real-world business scenarios, providing a practical learning experience that can be directly applied to your business.

Beyond the traditional routes of degrees and certifications, there are now many alternative education platforms that cater to entrepreneurs. Online platforms like Coursera, edX, and Udemy offer a wide range of courses that allow you to learn at your own pace and on your own schedule. These courses often cover specialized topics that can provide immediate value to your business, such as digital marketing, financial modeling, or coding for non-programmers. They also offer flexibility, allowing you to balance your education with the demands of running a business.

The Power of Informal Learning

While formal education is essential, informal learning is equally, if not more, important.

The beauty of informal learning is that it's self-directed and often more flexible. You can choose what to learn, how to learn it, and at what pace you want.

Books like this one are a great resource for informal learning. Many successful entrepreneurs are avid readers, constantly consuming literature on a wide range of topics. Whether it's business strategy, leadership, or even fiction, reading expands your mind and exposes you to new ideas and perspectives.

For example, books like *"The Lean Startup"* by Eric Ries, "Zero to One" by Peter Thiel, and "Good to Great" by Jim Collins are staples in the entrepreneurial world. These books provide insights into business strategies, innovation, and leadership that can be directly applied to your entrepreneurial journey.

In addition to business-focused books, reading biographies of successful entrepreneurs can provide valuable lessons and inspiration. Understanding the struggles, failures, and successes of those who have walked the path before you can be both motivating and educational.

Moreover, reading outside of your immediate field can offer new perspectives and creative ideas that you might not have considered otherwise. Books on psychology, history, art, or science can provide unique insights that apply to problem-solving, innovation, and leadership in your business. For example, studying historical leaders' strategies during times of crisis can inform how you approach challenges in your own business. Similarly, reading about scientific breakthroughs might inspire new ways to approach innovation and product development.

Podcasts and webinars are other valuable tools for informal learning. They allow you to gain insights from industry experts, often on very specific topics, and can be consumed on the go. Whether you're driving to a meeting, working out, or simply relaxing at home, podcasts offer a convenient way to continue your education.

Webinars and online workshops provide an interactive learning experience, often allowing you to ask questions and engage with the presenter. These sessions can be particularly valuable when they focus on niche topics relevant to your business, such as digital marketing trends, customer experience management, or legal aspects of entrepreneurship.

Additionally, TED Talks and other expert presentations available online can offer inspiration and insights from thought leaders across various industries. These talks often distill complex ideas into digestible, actionable advice, making them a valuable resource for any entrepreneur looking to expand their knowledge base.

Networking as a Learning Tool

Networking is often seen as a way to gain business connections, but it's also a powerful tool for learning. Engaging with other entrepreneurs, mentors, or industry experts can provide you with new perspectives, advice, and knowledge that you might not gain from traditional educational resources.

Consider joining entrepreneur groups or attending industry conferences. These environments are ripe with opportunities to learn from others' experiences and mistakes. You might find someone who has faced similar challenges and can offer advice on how to navigate them.

Networking also exposes you to new ideas and trends that you might not have encountered otherwise. By surrounding yourself with other driven, ambitious individuals, you're more likely to be exposed to the latest industry developments and innovative approaches to common challenges.

Moreover, networking can lead to collaborations and partnerships that can help your business grow. By learning from others and sharing your knowledge, you build relationships that can lead to new opportunities, whether it's a joint venture, a referral, or simply mutual support.

Engaging in online communities and forums can also be a valuable way to network and learn. Platforms like LinkedIn, Reddit, or industry-specific forums allow you to connect with professionals and experts from around the world. Participating in discussions, asking questions, and sharing your insights can help you build your reputation and expand your knowledge.

Finally, don't underestimate the value of networking within your local community. Local business groups, chambers of commerce, and entrepreneurial meetups provide opportunities to connect with other business owners in your area. These relationships can lead to collaborations, partnerships, and even new customers. Plus, local networking events often offer workshops and seminars that provide valuable learning opportunities.

Mental and Physical Well-being: The Foundation of Success

As an entrepreneur, it's easy to get caught up in the hustle and neglect your mental and physical health. However, your well-being is critical to your success. A healthy mind and body enable you to think clearly, make better decisions, and sustain the energy needed to run a business.

Prioritizing Mental Health

Mental health is often stigmatized in the business world, but it's crucial to acknowledge its importance. Stress, anxiety, and burnout are common among entrepreneurs, and if left unchecked, they can lead to serious consequences for both you and your business.

Investing in your mental health might mean different things to different people. For some, it could involve regular therapy sessions, while for others, it might be practicing mindfulness or meditation. The key is to find what works for you and make it a priority.

Mindfulness practices, such as meditation, have been shown to reduce stress, improve focus, and enhance overall well-being. Even just a few minutes of mindfulness each day can make a significant difference in your mental state. Apps like Headspace or Calm can guide you through these practices and help you establish a routine.

In addition to professional help, taking time for self-care is vital. Whether it's spending time with loved ones, pursuing hobbies, or simply taking breaks, these activities help you recharge and maintain a positive outlook.

Self-care isn't just about relaxation; it's about doing things that nurture your soul and keep you grounded. For some, this might be spending time in nature, while for others, it could be engaging in creative activities like painting, writing, or playing music. Whatever it is, make sure you carve out time for it regularly.

It's also important to recognize when you're feeling overwhelmed and to take steps to address it before it leads to burnout. This might mean delegating more tasks, saying no to additional responsibilities, or taking a short break to regroup.

In addition, regular exercise is a critical component of maintaining mental health. Physical activity releases endorphins, which are natural mood boosters. Whether it's a morning jog, a yoga class, or a dance session, regular physical activity can help you manage stress, anxiety, and depression. Many entrepreneurs find that maintaining a regular exercise routine helps them stay focused, energized, and resilient in the face of challenges.

Furthermore, maintaining a healthy work-life balance is crucial for mental well-being. As an entrepreneur, it's easy to become consumed by your business, working long hours and sacrificing personal time. However, this can lead to burnout and negatively impact both your mental health and your business performance.

Maintaining work-life balance involves setting boundaries and knowing when to step away from work. This could mean designating specific times for work and personal life, taking regular vacations, or simply unplugging from work-related devices after a certain hour each day. The time spent away from your business allows you to recharge, gain new perspectives, and return to work with renewed energy and focus.

Finally, it's important to build a support system that includes friends, family, and colleagues who understand the pressures of entrepreneurship and can offer emotional support. Having people to talk to, share your concerns with, and seek advice from can make a significant difference in your mental health.

Physical Health and Its Impact on Performance

Physical health is closely linked to mental health and overall performance. As an entrepreneur, maintaining your physical health should be a priority. This includes regular exercise, a balanced diet, and adequate sleep.

Exercise is not only good for your body but also for your mind. It improves your mood, increases your energy levels, and enhances your cognitive functions. Incorporating regular physical activity into your routine can help you stay sharp and focused, allowing you to tackle business challenges with greater efficiency.

Your diet also plays a crucial role in your physical health. A balanced diet that includes a variety of nutrients will provide you with the energy you need to stay productive throughout the day. Avoiding excessive caffeine, sugar, and processed foods can help prevent energy crashes and keep your mind clear.

Sleep is another essential component of physical health that is often neglected by entrepreneurs. Lack of sleep can impair your decision-making abilities, reduce your productivity, and negatively impact your mood. Prioritizing a regular sleep schedule and ensuring you get enough rest each night will help you stay alert, focused, and ready to take on the challenges of entrepreneurship.

Finally, regular check-ups and preventive healthcare are important for maintaining long-term physical health. As an entrepreneur, it's easy to put off doctor's visits and health screenings due to a busy schedule, but taking care of your health now can prevent more serious issues in the future.

Let's talk about The Value of Building a Personal Brand

In today's interconnected world, building a personal brand is an essential aspect of investing in yourself as an entrepreneur. Your personal brand is the reputation and image you project to the world, and it can significantly influence the success of your business.

Why Personal Branding Matters

A strong personal brand can set you apart from your competitors and establish you as an authority in your field. It can help you build trust with your audience, attract new opportunities, and even open doors that might otherwise be closed. In the digital age, where consumers and investors often research the people behind a brand before making decisions, having a well-crafted personal brand can be a significant asset.

Moreover, your personal brand is an extension of your business. It reflects your values, expertise, and the unique qualities that you bring to the table as an entrepreneur. By investing time and effort into building your personal brand, you not only enhance your own reputation but also add value to your business.

Steps to Building a Strong Personal Brand

Building a personal brand begins with self-reflection. Understand your strengths, values, and what sets you apart from others in your industry. What are you passionate about? What unique insights or experiences do you bring to your business? By identifying these key elements, you can begin to craft a personal brand that authentically represents who you are.

Next, establish a strong online presence. In today's digital world, your online presence is often the first impression people have of you. This includes your website, social media profiles, and any content you publish online. Ensure that all your online platforms consistently reflect your personal brand and values.

Content creation is a powerful tool for building your personal brand. Whether it's blogging, podcasting, or creating videos, sharing your knowledge and expertise with your audience helps establish you as an authority in your field. Consistent, high-quality content can attract followers, engage your audience, and ultimately drive more traffic to your business.

Networking also plays a crucial role in building your personal brand. Engage with others in your industry, attend events, and participate in discussions both online and offline. By being visible and active in your community, you reinforce your personal brand and expand your network.

Public speaking is another effective way to build your personal brand. Speaking at conferences, webinars, or industry events allows you to showcase your expertise and connect with a wider audience. It also positions you as a thought leader in your field, further enhancing your personal brand.

Finally, be authentic. Authenticity is key to building a personal brand that resonates with your audience. People can tell when you're being genuine, and they're more likely to trust and connect with you if you're authentic. Stay true to your values and let your personality shine through in everything you do.

Next: Financial Investment in Personal Growth

Investing in yourself also involves financial investment. This might mean spending money on courses, books, coaching, or even tools that help you grow as an entrepreneur. While it can be tempting to cut corners and save money, especially in the early stages of your business, it's important to recognize that investing in your personal growth is an investment in your business's future.

Allocating Resources Wisely

When deciding where to invest your resources, prioritize areas that will have the greatest impact on your growth and your business. This might involve hiring a coach or mentor who can guide you through challenges, or investing in courses that will provide you with the skills you need to grow your business.

It's also worth investing in tools and technology that can streamline your work and free up time for you to focus on growth. Whether it's project management software, customer relationship management (CRM) systems, or automation tools, these investments can increase your efficiency and allow you to scale your business more effectively.

Additionally, consider investing in your personal well-being. This could mean a gym membership, a healthy meal delivery service, or even a vacation to recharge. Remember, your well-being is directly linked to your business's success, so taking care of yourself is a worthwhile investment.

The Long-Term Benefits

The benefits of investing in yourself may not always be immediately apparent, but they are long-lasting. The knowledge and skills you acquire will serve you throughout your entrepreneurial journey, and the relationships you build through networking and personal branding can lead to opportunities years down the line.

Furthermore, investing in your well-being ensures that you have the stamina and resilience to navigate the ups and downs of entrepreneurship. The healthier and more balanced you are, the better equipped you'll be to handle challenges and seize opportunities as they arise.

Conclusion: A Lifelong Commitment to Growth

Investing in yourself is not a one-time event; it's a lifelong commitment. As an entrepreneur, you will face new challenges and opportunities at every stage of your journey, and your ability to adapt and grow will determine your long-term success.

By prioritizing continuous learning, maintaining your mental and physical health, building a strong personal brand, and making smart financial investments in your personal growth, you lay a solid foundation for both your personal and business success. Remember, the most valuable asset in your business is you. By investing in yourself, you ensure that your business has the best possible chance of thriving in the ever-changing world of entrepreneurship.

So, as you continue on your entrepreneurial journey, never stop investing in yourself. Stay curious, stay healthy, and stay true to your values and your success will thank you for it.

5

The Power of Knowing Your Value

"When you know your worth, you stop offering discounts."

In the world of entrepreneurship, success often hinges on a deep understanding of value—your value, your product's value, and the value you bring to the market. The most successful entrepreneurs aren't necessarily those with the most innovative ideas or the largest initial investments. Instead, they're often those who understand, articulate, and leverage their value with unwavering confidence. But what does it really mean to "know your value," and how can this knowledge be a game-changer in your entrepreneurial journey?

Knowing that what you have right now.. today.. is already of value -you don't have to wait to all of a sudden become valuable. Know your worth. Know that what you got today is just as valuable as what the future is about to hold.

These are the core foundational moments in life that are a necessity to building the next part of your dream. This foundational moment is just as valuable as the pictures of a finished product. Now I believe we are always growing, but I hope you understand what I mean.

If we are to take away the moments of the "now" that are preparing us for the moments of what's next, are we just building our house on the sand?

There is no skipping steps.

Change your mindset, change your actions, change your life.

One cannot just simply go from changing of a mindset and expect to have a change of life. You must change your actions.

There are no skipping steps.

You go to these mega-camps and these conferences and seminars and meet thousands of people that pump you up and inspire you, which I absolutely think we should go to more.

It's then though you go along your way and you have a change of mind. But you never go and change your actions and you expect to just have a change of life like that.

That will never work unfortunately, it just won't.

I'm just being honest.

I'm sitting here today writing this book because I went to a conference and a successful coach that's close to me challenged us to do something big.

Now I say that because he can challenge us all he wants. If I never change my actions, my life will never be changed.

I look back at this book now. I'm so thankful he challenged us to do something big. I've changed my actions, and now my life is changing.

Know your value,

Dont wait,

Now is the time!

I remember when I used to teach music professionally.

I knew a lot about music, but found myself really not progressing to my full potential.

The more I could teach it, the more I learned.

If you can't teach it, you really don't know it.

That's just the facts.

The more I teached, the more I knew. The more money I could charge!

The Power Of Knowing Your Value!

Understanding Your Value: The Foundation of Success

The journey of entrepreneurship begins with self-awareness. Knowing your value is about more than just putting a price tag on your services or products. It's about understanding what you uniquely bring to the table. What sets you apart from others in your field? What experiences, skills, and insights do you have that no one else can replicate?

This self-awareness is critical. It allows you to position yourself effectively in the market, targeting the right customers who need and appreciate what you offer. It's the difference between competing on price and competing on quality, expertise, or innovation. But self-awareness doesn't happen overnight; it's a continuous process of introspection and evaluation.

To truly understand your value, start by reflecting on your journey. What led you to become an entrepreneur? What challenges have you overcome? What successes have you achieved? These experiences shape not only your personal growth but also the unique value you offer to others. For example, if you've overcome significant obstacles to build your business, that resilience becomes part of your value proposition. It's something you bring to every client interaction, every project, and every decision you make.

Additionally, understanding your value involves recognizing your strengths and weaknesses. This can be challenging because it requires brutal honesty with yourself. Entrepreneurs often fall into the trap of thinking they need to be good at everything. However, true strength lies in recognizing where you excel and where you need help. By identifying your core competencies, you can focus on what you do best and seek out support in areas where you're less proficient.

Consider conducting a personal SWOT analysis—identifying your Strengths, Weaknesses, Opportunities, and Threats. This exercise can provide clarity on where your true value lies. Strengths are the qualities that set you apart—perhaps it's your ability to innovate, your deep industry knowledge, or your exceptional leadership skills. Weaknesses, on the other hand, might be areas where you lack experience or confidence. Opportunities are the external factors you can leverage to enhance your value, while threats are challenges that could undermine your efforts.

Understanding your value also means recognizing the value of your time. Time is one of the most precious resources for any entrepreneur. How you choose to spend it reflects your priorities and, ultimately, your value. Are you investing time in activities that align with your strengths and strategic goals, or are you getting bogged down in tasks that could be delegated or outsourced? By assessing where your time is best spent, you can make more informed decisions that enhance your overall value.

Articulating Your Value: Crafting a Compelling Narrative

Once you understand your value, the next step is to communicate it clearly and confidently. This isn't just about marketing—it's about crafting a narrative that resonates with your audience. Whether you're pitching to investors, negotiating with suppliers, or selling to customers, the ability to articulate your value can make or break the deal.

Articulating your value involves more than just listing your qualifications or features. It's about telling a compelling story that highlights the impact you can have on your client's life or business. It's about showing them not just what you do, but why it matters. This story should be consistent across all your communications, from your website and social media to your elevator pitch.

To create this narrative, start by identifying your target audience. Who are they? What are their needs, pain points, and desires? Understanding your audience is key to tailoring your message in a way that resonates with them. For example, if you're targeting small business owners, your value proposition might focus on how your services can help them save time, reduce costs, or grow their revenue.

Next, consider the emotional aspect of your value proposition. People make decisions based on emotions as much as logic, if not more. How does your product or service make your customers feel? Do you offer peace of mind, excitement, confidence, or relief? By tapping into these emotional triggers, you can create a more compelling and memorable narrative.

Another crucial aspect of articulating your value is differentiating yourself from the competition. In a crowded market, it's not enough to be good—you need to be different. What makes you unique? Perhaps it's your approach, your customer service, or your innovative use of technology. Whatever it is, make sure it's front and center in your narrative. Highlighting what makes you different helps potential customers understand why they should choose you over others.

In addition to differentiation, credibility is key. Back up your claims with evidence—whether it's customer testimonials, case studies, or data-driven results. For instance, if you claim that your product can increase efficiency by 20%, provide examples or statistics that support this claim. Credibility builds trust, and trust is essential for converting prospects into loyal customers.

Your narrative should also be adaptable to different contexts. The way you communicate your value to an investor will be different from how you present it to a potential client. For investors, you might focus on the financial upside and scalability of your business, while for clients, you might emphasize the tangible benefits they'll receive. Tailoring your message to your audience shows that you understand their needs and are focused on delivering value to them.

Lastly, remember that articulating your value is not a one-time task; it's an ongoing process. As your business evolves, so too should your narrative. Continuously refine your message based on feedback, market changes, and new insights. The more you communicate your value, the more confident you'll become, and the stronger your narrative will be.

Leveraging Your Value: Turning Knowledge into Action

Knowing and articulating your value are essential, but the true power comes from leveraging it effectively. This means using your value as a foundation for decision-making, pricing, and growth strategies.

For instance, if you know that your expertise is in high demand and scarce in the market, you can set your prices accordingly. You don't have to compete with lower-cost providers because you're offering something they can't—a unique perspective, a proven track record, or a specialized skill set. This approach not only enhances your profitability but also positions you as a premium option in the market.

Leveraging your value also involves knowing when to say no. Not every opportunity is worth pursuing, especially if it doesn't align with your value proposition. Being selective allows you to focus on the opportunities that best align with your strengths and where you can deliver the most value, ultimately leading to greater success.

Consider the concept of opportunity cost—the idea that choosing one opportunity means forgoing others.

As an entrepreneur, your time, energy, and resources are limited. By saying yes to one project, you're effectively saying no to others. Therefore, it's crucial to assess whether each opportunity aligns with your core value and strategic goals. Does it allow you to leverage your strengths? Will it enhance your reputation or open doors to further opportunities? If not, it might be wise to pass.

Pricing is another area where knowing your value is crucial. Many entrepreneurs struggle with pricing their products or services, often undercharging out of fear of losing business. However, pricing is not just about covering costs or beating competitors—it's about reflecting the value you provide. If you offer something unique, whether it's a specialized service, a premium product, or exceptional customer support, your prices should reflect that value.

Consider a luxury brand like Rolex. Customers are not just buying a watch; they're buying a symbol of status, craftsmanship, and exclusivity. The high price tag is a reflection of the brand's perceived value. Similarly, if you position your product or service as premium, your pricing should reinforce that perception. It's important to remember that price is often associated with quality—charging too little can undermine your credibility and devalue your offering.

Leveraging your value also extends to building strategic partnerships. As an entrepreneur, your network is one of your most valuable assets. By aligning yourself with partners who complement your strengths and share your values, you can create synergies that enhance your value proposition. For example, if you're a software developer, partnering with a design expert could allow you to offer a more comprehensive solution to clients. Such partnerships can lead to new opportunities, increased visibility, and a stronger market position.

Growth strategies should also be rooted in your understanding of value. As your business expands, it's important to stay true to the core value that made you successful in the first place. Diversification can be a powerful growth strategy, but it should be approached with caution. Expanding into new markets or offering new products can dilute your value proposition if not done thoughtfully. Before branching out, ask yourself whether the new venture aligns with your strengths and whether it enhances or detracts from your existing value.

One way to maintain focus as you grow is to develop a clear value-based mission statement. This statement should encapsulate what you stand for and guide your decision-making process. For example, if your mission is to provide innovative, high-quality solutions to your customers, any new initiative should be evaluated against this mission. Does it contribute to innovation? Does it maintain or enhance quality? If not, it may not be the right path to pursue.

The Confidence to Demand Your Worth: Overcoming Challenges

One of the most challenging aspects of entrepreneurship is having the confidence to demand what you're worth. This is where many entrepreneurs falter, either undervaluing themselves out of fear of losing business or overvaluing themselves without the substance to back it up.

Confidence comes from a deep belief in your value. When you know what you bring to the table, you're less likely to settle for less than you're worth. This confidence is contagious—it reassures clients, attracts investors, and solidifies partnerships. However, confidence is not something that comes naturally to everyone. It's often built through experience, self-reflection, and a series of small wins that reinforce your belief in your abilities.

One way to build confidence is to regularly review your accomplishments. Keep a journal or a portfolio of your successes, whether it's a major project you completed, positive feedback from a client, or a challenging situation you navigated successfully. Reviewing these achievements can serve as a reminder of your value, especially during times of doubt.

Another key to confidence is preparation. Whether you're negotiating a contract, pitching to investors, or presenting to clients, being well-prepared can significantly boost your confidence. This means not only knowing your value but also understanding the needs and expectations of the other party. The more prepared you are, the more confident you'll feel in asserting your worth.

However, confidence should not be confused with arrogance. True confidence is grounded in reality. It's about recognizing both your strengths and your limitations, and knowing how to leverage the former while addressing the latter. Arrogance, on the other hand, is an overestimation of one's abilities, often coupled with a dismissal of others' perspectives. While confidence attracts, arrogance repels. It's important to strike a balance where you are assertive about your value, yet open to feedback and willing to learn.

One common pitfall is the fear of rejection, which can lead entrepreneurs to undervalue themselves. This fear often stems from a scarcity mindset—the belief that opportunities are limited and that any lost opportunity is a major setback. However, this mindset can be counterproductive. By underpricing yourself or accepting unfavorable terms, you might win the business, but you could also end up overworked, underpaid, and resentful.

Shifting to an abundance mindset can help overcome this fear. This mindset is based on the belief that opportunities are plentiful and that you don't have to compromise your value to succeed. It encourages you to pursue opportunities that align with your value proposition and to walk away from those that don't. It's about playing the long game—focusing on building a sustainable, profitable business rather than just chasing immediate gains.

Lastly, confidence to demand your worth also involves setting boundaries. As an entrepreneur, it's easy to fall into the trap of saying yes to everything, especially in the early stages when you're eager to grow your business. However, overcommitting can lead to burnout and can dilute your value proposition. Setting boundaries means being clear about what you will and won't do, and sticking to it. This might involve setting minimum project fees, limiting the number of clients you take on at once, or being clear about your availability.

Conclusion: Transforming Your Entrepreneurial Journey

The power of knowing your value as an entrepreneur cannot be overstated. It's the foundation upon which you build your business, the key to effective communication, and the driving force behind your pricing and growth strategies. By understanding, articulating, and leveraging your value, you position yourself to not just compete in your market, but to lead it.

In the end, the most successful entrepreneurs are those who don't just know their worth—they demand it. And in doing so, they create businesses that are not just profitable, but also meaningful and impactful. So, take the time to deeply understand your value, communicate it with clarity and confidence, and watch as it transforms your entrepreneurial journey.

This journey is not without its challenges, but by consistently aligning your actions with your value, you'll find that these challenges become opportunities for growth and innovation. Knowing your value is not just about achieving business success—it's about building a life and career that reflect who you truly are and what you stand for. When you operate from this place of alignment and authenticity, you not only succeed on your terms, but you also inspire others to do the same.

Embrace the power of knowing your value. Let it guide you, motivate you, and empower you to achieve your highest potential as an entrepreneur. The path may not always be easy, but with a clear understanding of your value, you will have the resilience and confidence to overcome obstacles and create a lasting impact.

6

The Benefit of Adding Value to Others

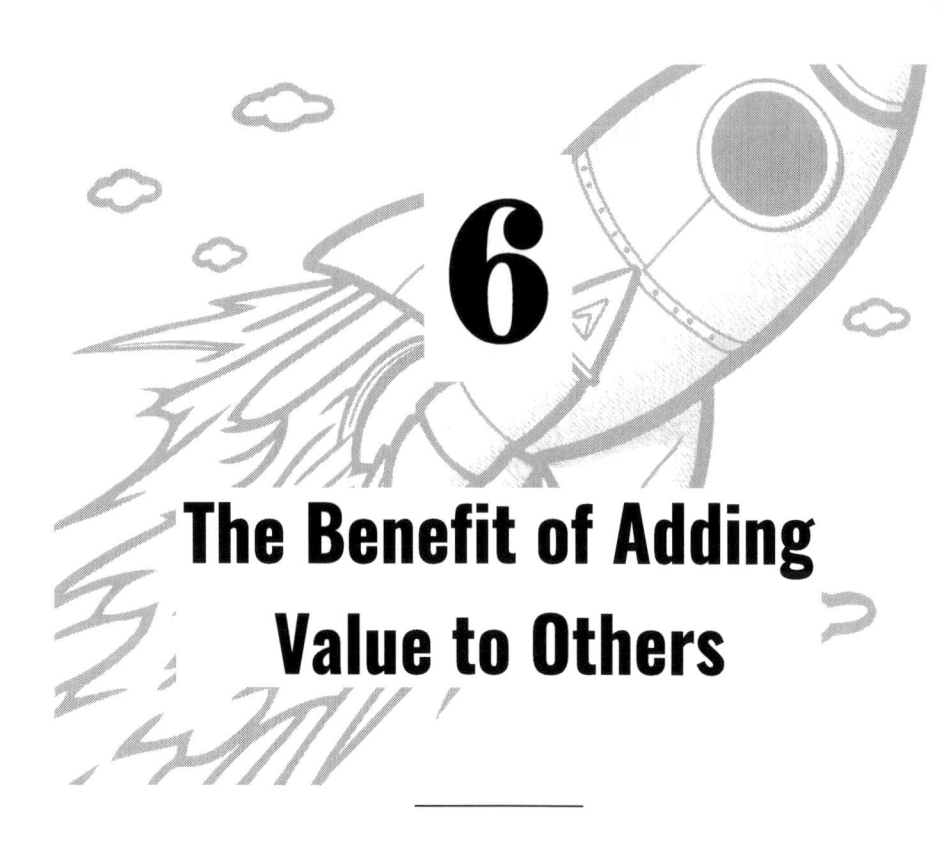

"When you focus on adding value to others, your own success will follow naturally."

The True Measure of Success

In the high-paced world of entrepreneurship, where deals, profits, and market shares dominate conversations, it's easy to lose sight of the core principles that lead to sustainable success. Often, entrepreneurs are so focused on their bottom line that they forget one of the most powerful drivers of success: adding value to others. This chapter delves deep into why adding value to others is not just a strategic move but a vital part of long-lasting success and personal fulfillment. It explores the profound impact of this principle on relationships, reputation, and business growth, offering insights and practical advice on how to integrate this approach into your entrepreneurial journey.

The Foundation of Strong Relationships

In business, as in life, the strength of your relationships often determines the extent of your success. When you make it your mission to add value to others, you're investing in these relationships in a meaningful way. These investments might not yield immediate returns, but they build the foundation for long-term success.

The Power of Authentic Connections:

Authentic connections are the bedrock of successful entrepreneurship. In a world where business is often transactional, authenticity sets you apart. By genuinely adding value to others—whether it's through sharing knowledge, offering support, or simply being there when needed—you create connections that transcend mere business relationships. These connections evolve into partnerships, alliances, and networks that can propel your business to new heights. People do business with those they know, like, and trust, and nothing builds trust more effectively than consistently adding value to others' lives.

The Role of Emotional Intelligence:

Emotional intelligence (EQ) plays a significant role in building and maintaining relationships. Understanding the emotions, needs, and motivations of others allows you to add value in a way that resonates deeply. Entrepreneurs with high EQ are often more successful because they know how to connect with others on a personal level, creating a sense of empathy and understanding that goes beyond business. By honing your EQ, you can better assess how to add value in each interaction, whether it's with a client, a partner, or an employee.

Building a Network of Support:

Your network is your net worth. By consistently adding value to others, you build a network of support that can help you overcome challenges, seize opportunities, and navigate the complexities of entrepreneurship. This network isn't just about professional connections; it's about creating a community of people who are invested in your success because you've been invested in theirs. This mutual support system is invaluable, especially in times of uncertainty or when you're venturing into uncharted territory.

The Law of Reciprocity: A Cornerstone of Success

One of the fundamental principles of adding value is the law of reciprocity. This law states that when you help others, they feel a natural inclination to help you in return. While this might seem like a simple concept, its implications are profound and far-reaching.

The Ethical Dimension of Reciprocity:

It's important to approach the law of reciprocity with the right mindset. Adding value should never be about manipulation or expecting something in return. Instead, it's about creating a culture of generosity and goodwill. When you help others without any expectation of repayment, you're fostering a positive environment where everyone feels supported. Over time, this environment encourages a cycle of giving and receiving that benefits everyone involved. The key is to give freely, with no strings attached, knowing that the goodwill you generate will come back to you in ways you might not expect.

Practical Applications in Business:

In business, the law of reciprocity can take many forms. It might mean offering free advice or resources to a potential client, mentoring a less experienced entrepreneur, or going above and beyond to ensure a customer's satisfaction. These actions, though seemingly small, create a reservoir of goodwill that you can draw upon when needed. Over time, this approach not only strengthens your relationships but also enhances your reputation as someone who adds value, making you a go-to person in your industry.

Case Study: Reciprocity in Action:

Consider the story of a young entrepreneur who started a small marketing agency. Instead of focusing solely on landing paying clients, she spent her first year offering free workshops to small businesses in her community. These workshops were designed to add value, providing practical tips and strategies that business owners could implement immediately. While she didn't make much money initially, her reputation as an expert and a giver grew rapidly. When these businesses eventually needed more extensive marketing services, they turned to her agency because she had already established trust and added value to their lives. This is the power of reciprocity in action.

Contribution Over Compensation: A Paradigm Shift

Entrepreneurship often involves a delicate balance between giving and receiving. However, one of the most significant challenges for many entrepreneurs is shifting their mindset from compensation to contribution. This shift is not just philosophical; it's a practical approach that can have a profound impact on your business.

The Psychology of Contribution:

Psychologically, humans are wired to seek rewards, which is why the idea of compensation is so ingrained in business. However, studies have shown that those who focus on contribution rather than compensation tend to experience greater long-term success and personal fulfillment. This is because the act of giving triggers positive emotions and creates a sense of purpose. For entrepreneurs, this sense of purpose can be a powerful motivator, driving them to push through challenges and stay committed to their vision.

The Ripple Effect of Contribution:

When you contribute to others without expecting anything in return, you create a ripple effect that extends far beyond the initial act. This ripple effect can manifest in various ways—through word-of-mouth referrals, opportunities that arise unexpectedly, or the goodwill that spreads through your network. The key to harnessing this ripple effect is consistency. By making contribution a regular part of your business strategy, you ensure that these positive ripples continue to expand, bringing more opportunities and success your way.

From Transactional to Transformational Relationships:

By focusing on contribution, you shift your relationships from being transactional to transformational. Transactional relationships are based on an exchange of value—what you can get in return for what you give. Transformational relationships, on the other hand, are based on mutual growth and development. When you approach relationships with a mindset of contribution, you're not just looking to get something in return; you're looking to create something greater together. This approach leads to more meaningful and fulfilling partnerships, whether they're with clients, employees, or other entrepreneurs.

Everyday Acts of Value: The Little Things That Matter

Adding value doesn't always require grand gestures or significant investments. Often, it's the small, everyday actions that leave the most lasting impression. These actions might seem insignificant at the moment, but they can have a profound impact on the people you interact with and on your business as a whole.

The Importance of Mindfulness in Adding Value:

Mindfulness plays a crucial role in identifying opportunities to add value. By being present and attentive in your interactions, you can pick up on small cues that others might miss. This attentiveness allows you to offer help or support in ways that are meaningful and impactful. Whether it's a word of encouragement, a thoughtful gesture, or simply taking the time to listen, these small acts of value contribute to a positive experience for the other person, which they are likely to remember and appreciate.

Real-Life Examples of Everyday Value:

Consider the example of a customer service representative who goes out of their way to solve a customer's problem, even if it means bending the rules a little. This small act of value can turn a dissatisfied customer into a loyal one. Or think about an entrepreneur who takes the time to send a handwritten thank-you note to a client after a successful project. These small gestures may not seem like much, but they create a lasting impression and reinforce the idea that you care about more than just business—you care about the people you work with.

The Compounding Effect of Small Actions:

The compounding effect of small actions can't be underestimated. Each small act of value contributes to a larger narrative about who you are and what you stand for. Over time, these actions build up, creating a strong reputation and a network of people who respect and trust you. This compounding effect is one of the most powerful tools in an entrepreneur's arsenal, and it's something that can be leveraged in every aspect of your business.

Building a Reputation of Value

Your reputation is one of your most valuable assets as an entrepreneur. It precedes you in every interaction, and it's built on the value you add to others. A strong reputation can open doors, create opportunities, and provide a competitive advantage in the marketplace.

The Role of Consistency in Building Reputation:

Consistency is key when it comes to building a reputation of value. It's not enough to add value occasionally or when it's convenient; you need to make it a consistent part of your business practices. This means looking for opportunities to add value in every interaction, whether it's with a client, a partner, or even a competitor. Consistent value-adding behavior builds trust and credibility, both of which are essential for a strong reputation.

Leveraging Reputation for Business Growth:

Once you've built a reputation as someone who adds value, you can leverage it to grow your business. A strong reputation attracts clients, partners, and investors who want to work with someone they can trust. It also makes it easier to negotiate deals, close sales, and expand your network. In essence, your reputation becomes a self-reinforcing asset that drives your business forward.

Case Study: The Value of a Strong Reputation:

Let's take the example of a well-known entrepreneur who started with a small tech startup. From the beginning, he focused on adding value to his customers by providing exceptional service and innovative solutions. Over time, his reputation as a value-driven entrepreneur spread, attracting top talent to his team and high-profile investors to his company. His startup eventually became a major player in the tech industry, largely due to the strong reputation he built through his commitment to adding value.

The Ripple Effect of Value

The concept of the ripple effect illustrates how small actions can have far-reaching consequences. When you add value to others, you create a ripple that extends through your network and beyond, amplifying the impact of your efforts.

Creating a Culture of Value:

One of the most powerful ways to harness the ripple effect is by creating a culture of value within your organization. When you instill this culture in your team, everyone is motivated to add value in their interactions with clients, partners, and each other. This collective effort amplifies the impact of each individual's contributions, creating a positive feedback loop that benefits everyone involved.

The Global Impact of Local Actions:

The ripple effect isn't limited to your immediate network; it can extend to a global scale. For example, a small business that practices sustainable and ethical sourcing can inspire others to follow suit, creating a larger movement towards responsible business practices. Similarly, a company that prioritizes social responsibility can influence industry standards and consumer behavior. The actions you take to add value can have a broader impact, shaping trends and inspiring change on a larger scale.

Measuring the Impact of the Ripple Effect:

While the ripple effect is often intangible, it's important to recognize and measure its impact. This can be done through feedback from clients, tracking referrals and word-of-mouth recommendations, and assessing the overall growth and success of your business. By understanding the impact of your value-adding efforts, you can better appreciate the long-term benefits and continue to invest in this approach.

The Impact on Your Business

Adding value has tangible benefits for your business, affecting various aspects from customer loyalty to team productivity. By focusing on adding value, you create a solid foundation for growth and success.

Increased Customer Loyalty:

One of the most significant benefits of adding value is increased customer loyalty. When customers feel valued and supported, they're more likely to stay loyal to your brand. This loyalty translates into repeat business, positive reviews, and referrals, all of which are crucial for long-term success. By consistently adding value, you turn one-time customers into lifelong advocates for your business.

Enhanced Team Morale and Productivity:

The principle of adding value extends to your internal team as well. When you focus on supporting and developing your team members, you create a positive work environment that boosts morale and productivity. Employees who feel valued are more engaged and motivated, leading to higher performance and better business outcomes. Investing in your team's growth and well-being pays off in the form of increased efficiency and a more cohesive work culture.

Stronger Partnerships and Collaborations:

In the business world, partnerships and collaborations are often key to success. By approaching these relationships with a mindset of adding value, you create stronger, more productive partnerships. This approach fosters a collaborative environment where both parties benefit and contribute to each other's success. Strong partnerships can lead to joint ventures, shared resources, and new opportunities, all of which can drive your business forward.

Long-Term Business Growth:

Adding value is a long-term strategy that contributes to sustainable business growth. Unlike short-term tactics that may yield immediate results but fade over time, adding value creates a solid foundation for ongoing success. By focusing on how you can contribute to others' success, you build a network of support, a strong reputation, and loyal customers—all of which are essential for long-term business growth.

Conclusion: The Legacy of Value

As you navigate your entrepreneurial journey, keep in mind that success is not just about what you achieve for yourself but about the legacy you leave behind. Adding value to others is a powerful way to create a lasting impact, not only on your business but on the world around you.

Building a Lasting Legacy:

The legacy you build through adding value extends beyond financial success. It encompasses the relationships you've forged, the positive changes you've inspired, and the lives you've touched. This legacy becomes a testament to your character and your commitment to making a difference. It's a legacy that can inspire future generations of entrepreneurs and leave a mark on your industry and community.

The Fulfillment of Value:

Ultimately, adding value brings a sense of fulfillment that goes beyond financial rewards. It's about knowing that your efforts have made a positive difference in the lives of others. This sense of purpose and satisfaction is what drives many successful entrepreneurs to continue their work with passion and dedication. By focusing on adding value, you align your business with a greater purpose, creating a meaningful and rewarding entrepreneurial journey.

In conclusion, the measure of your success as an entrepreneur is deeply intertwined with the value you add to others. By making it your mission to contribute, support, and uplift those around you, you create a ripple effect that not only enhances your business but also leaves a lasting legacy. Embrace this principle as a core part of your entrepreneurial strategy, and you'll find that success follows naturally, enriching both your professional and personal life.

7

The Power of Being Skeptical

"Question everything; skepticism is the guardrail that keeps you from falling into complacency."

In the high-stakes world of entrepreneurship, optimism is often celebrated as a core trait of successful leaders. The ability to envision a brighter future, to see potential where others see obstacles, and to maintain unwavering belief in one's ideas can be crucial. However, while optimism can propel an entrepreneur forward, it is the careful balance with skepticism that can often determine success or failure.

Skepticism: The Undervalued Virtue

Skepticism is not about being negative or pessimistic; it's about questioning assumptions, probing deeper into details, and ensuring that decisions are based on facts, not just hope or hype. In the early stages of building a business, this trait is especially valuable. It is easy to get caught up in excitement—whether it's about a new product idea, a potential market opportunity, or a partnership that seems perfect on paper. However, as an entrepreneur, your job is to critically assess these opportunities and risks before diving in headfirst.

Entrepreneurs, by nature, are visionaries. They see what others cannot and have the courage to chase their dreams. Yet, the same qualities that make an entrepreneur bold can also blind them to the realities that could derail their ventures. This is where skepticism comes into play. It acts as a counterbalance to the unbridled enthusiasm that often accompanies new ideas and opportunities. Skepticism requires you to step back and scrutinize every aspect of your plan—challenging the assumptions you hold, the data you rely on, and the very premise of your business model.

Why Skepticism Matters

At its core, skepticism helps entrepreneurs avoid the traps of wishful thinking. While it's important to believe in your vision, it's equally important to rigorously test that vision against reality. For example, when launching a new product, a healthy dose of skepticism can prompt you to question whether there's truly a market for it, whether your target customers will actually pay for it, or whether the competition is stronger than you initially thought.

Too often, entrepreneurs fall in love with their ideas and overlook red flags that could have been addressed early on. By being skeptical, you force yourself to seek out these potential issues before they become costly mistakes. This doesn't mean you should be paralyzed by doubt, but rather that you should approach each decision with a critical mind and a willingness to dig deeper.

Skepticism also plays a crucial role in managing expectations—both your own and those of your stakeholders. Investors, partners, and employees often look to entrepreneurs for guidance and confidence. While it's essential to project optimism, it's equally important to temper that optimism with realism. Overpromising and underdelivering can erode trust and damage your reputation. By practicing skepticism, you can set more realistic goals, provide accurate projections, and build a foundation of trust with those who are counting on your leadership.

The Risks of Unchecked Optimism

Unchecked optimism can be just as dangerous as unchecked skepticism. When you are overly optimistic, you may overlook warning signs, dismiss valid concerns, or rush into decisions without fully understanding the risks. This can lead to costly mistakes, such as entering a saturated market, investing too heavily in unproven technology, or partnering with unreliable stakeholders.

In contrast, a healthy dose of skepticism can serve as a protective mechanism, helping you to avoid these pitfalls. By questioning your assumptions and challenging your own ideas, you can identify potential risks before they become insurmountable obstacles. This doesn't mean you should be paralyzed by fear or doubt, but rather that you should be deliberate and methodical in your decision-making process.

For instance, consider the process of securing funding for your business. Optimism might lead you to believe that every investor pitch will result in a check, or that your initial valuation is justified by your enthusiasm for the business. Skepticism, however, would prompt you to consider the investor's perspective: Are the financial projections realistic? Is there a solid exit strategy? Are there potential flaws in the business model that could be exposed under scrutiny? By approaching the fundraising process with a healthy level of skepticism, you are more likely to present a compelling and realistic case to potential investors, thereby increasing your chances of securing the necessary capital.

Building a Skeptical Mindset

Developing a skeptical mindset begins with recognizing that not every idea, trend, or piece of advice is worth pursuing. Start by questioning the assumptions that underpin your business. Ask yourself:

- What evidence do I have that this idea will work?
- What are the potential downsides, and how can I mitigate them?
- Am I relying too heavily on my own biases or the opinions of others?
- What would I do if this assumption proved wrong?

Encourage your team to do the same. Create an environment where challenging ideas is not only accepted but encouraged. This doesn't mean fostering negativity, but rather cultivating a culture where the best ideas rise to the top because they've been thoroughly vetted and tested.

Building a skeptical mindset is also about developing intellectual humility—the willingness to admit that you might be wrong and the openness to changing your mind when presented with new evidence. Intellectual humility is a hallmark of great leaders because it allows them to pivot when necessary, rather than stubbornly clinging to ideas or strategies that aren't working.

One practical way to cultivate skepticism within your organization is to establish a "devil's advocate" role during strategic discussions. This person's job is to challenge the prevailing assumptions and raise potential objections. By institutionalizing this practice, you create a culture where questioning is not only tolerated but valued as a critical part of the decision-making process.

The Role of Data and Research

One of the best tools at your disposal as an entrepreneur is data. Being skeptical means relying on evidence to inform your decisions, not just gut feelings. Before committing to a strategy, look for data that supports your hypothesis. If you're entering a new market, study the market trends, analyze the competition, and gather customer feedback. Use this information to refine your approach and reduce uncertainty.

It's also important to stay current with industry research and trends. The entrepreneurial landscape is constantly shifting, and what worked last year might not work now. By maintaining a healthy skepticism about your business's position in the market, you can pivot more quickly and adapt to changes before they negatively impact your bottom line.

In the age of big data, entrepreneurs have more information at their fingertips than ever before. However, data is only as valuable as the insights you can extract from it. This is where skepticism is crucial. It's not enough to simply collect data; you must also analyze it critically, looking for patterns, anomalies, and correlations that may challenge your assumptions. By doing so, you can make more informed decisions, mitigate risks, and seize opportunities that others might overlook.

For example, if you're considering launching a new product, don't just rely on market research reports that support your hypothesis. Dig deeper into the data: What are the historical trends in this market? Are there seasonal fluctuations that could affect demand? How do customer preferences vary across different segments? By asking these questions and analyzing the data from multiple angles, you can gain a more nuanced understanding of the market and make smarter decisions.

Balancing Skepticism with Optimism

While skepticism is a powerful tool, it should not overshadow the optimism that fuels entrepreneurial drive. The key is finding the right balance between the two. Too much skepticism can lead to paralysis by analysis, where you spend so much time questioning every detail that you fail to take action. On the other hand, unchecked optimism can result in taking unnecessary risks or pursuing ventures that are doomed to fail.

Successful entrepreneurs learn to balance these two mindsets. They dream big and push boundaries, but they do so with a critical eye and a commitment to reality. They are not afraid to pivot when the data suggests a change is needed, and they are not discouraged by skepticism; instead, they use it as a tool to refine their ideas and make smarter decisions.

Balancing skepticism and optimism is also about managing your emotional responses to both success and failure. When things are going well, it's easy to become complacent and assume that your success will continue indefinitely. Skepticism can help you avoid this trap by reminding you to stay vigilant and continue questioning your assumptions. Conversely, when you encounter setbacks, it's important to maintain your optimism and belief in your ability to overcome challenges. By keeping both skepticism and optimism in check, you can navigate the ups and downs of entrepreneurship with resilience and confidence.

Case Studies: When Skepticism Saved the Day

To further illustrate the power of skepticism, let's look at a few real-world examples where a healthy dose of skepticism made the difference between success and failure.

Case Study 1: The Dot-Com Bubble Burst

During the late 1990s, the dot-com boom saw a frenzy of investment in internet-based companies, many of which had little more than a business plan and a catchy name. Optimism was rampant, and investors were eager to pour money into any company with a ".com" in its name. However, those who approached the market with skepticism—questioning the viability of these business models, the overvaluation of companies, and the lack of revenue streams—were able to avoid the catastrophic losses that followed the burst of the bubble. These skeptics invested more cautiously, focusing on companies with solid fundamentals and realistic growth prospects, and ultimately emerged from the crash in a stronger position.

Case Study 2: The Rise of Netflix

In the early 2000s, when Netflix was still a DVD rental service, the company faced significant skepticism about its future. The idea of mailing DVDs to customers seemed quaint in the face of the rapidly growing Blockbuster empire, which dominated the video rental market. However, Netflix's founders, Reed Hastings and Marc Randolph, were skeptical of the long-term viability of physical rental stores and recognized the potential of online streaming. By questioning the prevailing industry wisdom and being skeptical of the traditional video rental model, Netflix was able to pivot to streaming, ultimately disrupting the entire industry and becoming the global powerhouse it is today.

Case Study 3: The Failure of Quibi

On the flip side, the short-lived streaming service Quibi is a cautionary tale of what happens when skepticism is ignored. Launched in 2020 with significant fanfare and nearly $2 billion in funding, Quibi was designed to deliver short-form video content tailored for mobile devices. The founders, Jeffrey Katzenberg and Meg Whitman, were optimistic that consumers would embrace this new format. However, they failed to adequately test their assumptions and did not listen to the skepticism from industry experts who questioned the platform's value proposition, content strategy, and timing (launching during a pandemic when people had more time for longer content). As a result, Quibi failed to gain traction and was shuttered just six months after its launch.

Conclusion: Embracing the Power of Skepticism

In the journey of entrepreneurship, skepticism is a powerful ally. It keeps you grounded, ensures your decisions are well-informed, and helps you navigate the complexities of building a business. By embracing skepticism, you can protect your business from pitfalls and position yourself to take advantage of genuine opportunities. Remember, it's not about doubting everything—it's about questioning enough to make sure you're on the right path.

As you continue to build and grow your business, let skepticism be the compass that guides you through the fog of uncertainty. Combined with optimism, it can help you chart a course that leads not only to success but to sustainable, long-term growth.

8

Don't Wait for the Right Time, NOW is the Time

"Waiting for the perfect moment is the enemy of progress; take action today, and perfection will follow."

The Illusion of the "The Right Time"

We've all heard it before: "I'm going to wait for the right moment." Or perhaps, "I'll get started when I have everything straightened out." Maybe you've even said, "I'm just waiting for all my ducks to be in a row." But here's the truth—if you're the kind of person who keeps saying, "I'm going to wait for the right time," you'll never find it. The so-called "right time" isn't coming. It doesn't exist.

The idea of the "the right time" is an illusion—a comforting narrative we tell ourselves to justify inaction. We think that one day, everything will align perfectly, and we'll feel completely ready to take that big leap. But life isn't a movie where all the pieces fall into place effortlessly. It's messy, unpredictable, and constantly evolving. Waiting for the perfect moment is like chasing a mirage; it's always just out of reach.

Entrepreneurs, especially those at the beginning of their journey, often fall into this trap. The desire to start on a solid foundation is understandable, but it can also be paralyzing. The more you plan, the more you realize how much there is to consider, and the more likely you are to find reasons not to begin. The reality is that the stars will never perfectly align. There will always be uncertainties, risks, and challenges, no matter how much you prepare. The difference between those who succeed and those who don't is often simply the willingness to take that first step despite the imperfections.

The Cost of Waiting

Every day you spend waiting for the right time is a day lost—a day you could have spent building your dreams, moving closer to your goals, and creating the life you desire. The cost of waiting isn't just time; it's opportunity. Each moment you hesitate, someone else is seizing the chance, learning, growing, and making progress. Time is the most valuable asset we have, and it's non-renewable. Once it's gone, it's gone forever.

That's just what it is.

Waiting also takes a toll on your confidence. The longer you wait, the more you doubt yourself. You start to believe that you're not capable, that the obstacles are too great, that maybe you're not cut out for the challenge. But these doubts are self-imposed limitations. The truth is, you'll never feel completely ready, and that's okay. The important thing is to start, to take that first step, no matter how small.

In the business world, there's a concept known as "opportunity cost"—the cost of what you forego when you choose one option over another. When you delay taking action, the opportunity cost can be immense. You miss out on potential growth, learning experiences, and market opportunities. In some cases, by the time you're ready to act, the window of opportunity has closed. Markets shift, consumer needs change, and what was once a groundbreaking idea becomes obsolete.

Furthermore, waiting can lead to analysis paralysis—a state where you overthink every detail to the point where you're unable to make a decision. You become so focused on what could go wrong that you lose sight of what could go right. This kind of over-analysis can be detrimental to entrepreneurs, as it prevents you from ever getting started. Remember, progress is made by doing, not by endlessly planning.

Embracing Imperfection

One of the main reasons people wait for the right time is the fear of imperfection. We want everything to be just right before we begin—a flawless plan, ideal circumstances, complete confidence. But perfection is a myth. It's an unattainable standard that paralyzes us and prevents us from taking action.

Successful entrepreneurs understand that imperfection is part of the process. They know that mistakes are inevitable and that failure is a necessary stepping stone to success. The key is not to avoid imperfection but to embrace it. Start where you are, with what you have, and improve along the way. Every mistake is a lesson, every setback is an opportunity to grow. The most successful people are those who are willing to start before they're ready, who understand that progress is better than perfection.

Take the example of product development in the tech industry. The most innovative companies don't wait to launch until they have a perfect product. Instead, they release a "minimum viable product" (MVP)—a basic version with just enough features to satisfy early adopters. They then gather feedback, iterate, and improve the product based on real user experiences. This approach not only speeds up time-to-market but also ensures that the final product is better aligned with customer needs.

In your own entrepreneurial journey, consider adopting a similar mindset. Rather than waiting until every detail is perfected, focus on getting your idea out into the world. You can refine and improve as you go. Remember, it's not about being perfect; it's about making progress.

The Power of Decision

Success requires action, not waiting. Sometimes, you have to set a date on the calendar and commit yourself to it. If you keep thinking there's some magic solution out there, a moment when everything will fall perfectly into place—whether it's your health, your financial status, or your social standing—you're mistaken. There isn't a magic age, a special time of year, or a secret program that's going to solve all your problems.

Making a decision is powerful. It's a declaration of intent, a commitment to yourself that you're going to make something happen. When you decide to act, you're taking control of your life and your future. You're no longer waiting for circumstances to be right; you're creating the circumstances you need. Decisions are the building blocks of success. Each decision you make moves you closer to your goals.

Consider the power of small decisions. Every day, you're faced with countless choices, from what time to wake up to how you spend your free time. These decisions, though seemingly insignificant, compound over time and shape the trajectory of your life. Successful entrepreneurs understand the importance of making decisions quickly and confidently. They know that indecision is the enemy of progress.

Think of the moments in your life when you made a decisive choice—whether it was to start a new job, launch a business, or end a relationship. These moments likely led to significant changes and growth. Now, imagine if you had waited for the "right time" to make those decisions. How different would your life be? The same applies to your entrepreneurial journey. Now I'm not saying you won't ever regain those relationships you thought were bad or end that new job you thought was a good job, what I am saying is, "the sooner you decide to act, the sooner you'll see results."

Confronting Excuses

We all have excuses. "I can't get healthy because I can't afford a personal trainer." "I can't start my business because I don't have the right connections." "I can't move forward until..." But this mindset is a trap. Excuses are convenient lies we tell ourselves to avoid discomfort, risk, and effort. They're the rationalizations that keep us in our comfort zone, away from the challenges that lead to growth.

But here's the thing—excuses don't solve problems. They don't move you forward. They don't bring you closer to your dreams. In fact, they do the opposite. They keep you stuck, stagnant, and unfulfilled. The longer you cling to your excuses, the further you drift from the life you want to live.

Entrepreneurs who succeed are those who refuse to be held back by excuses. They understand that every obstacle is an opportunity in disguise. Rather than saying, "I can't," they ask, "How can I?" They look for solutions, not problems. If they lack resources, they get creative. If they lack knowledge, they seek out mentors or learn on their own. They don't let excuses dictate their actions; instead, they use challenges as fuel for their determination.

Consider the story of Sara Blakely, the founder of Spanx. When she first came up with the idea for her revolutionary shapewear, she had no experience in the fashion industry, no formal business education, and very little money. But she didn't let these obstacles become excuses. Instead, she took action. She cut the feet off her pantyhose, created a prototype, and pitched her idea to manufacturers—many of whom rejected her. But she persisted, and today, Spanx is a billion-dollar company. Sara's story is a testament to the power of confronting excuses and taking action.

It's time to confront your excuses. Recognize them for what they are—barriers you've constructed to protect yourself from the fear of failure. And then, dismantle them. Replace them with reasons to act, with motivations to push forward. Remember, the more you wait, the less likely you are to start anything. Procrastination is a silent killer of dreams.

The Importance of Discipline

Let's be honest: laziness is often the root cause. That's a harsh truth, but it's one we need to hear. No one is coming to save you. No one is going to fix your problems, hand you a business plan, or remind you to brush your teeth every morning. The only person who can make it happen is you.

Discipline is the cornerstone of success. It's the ability to do what needs to be done, even when you don't feel like doing it. It's waking up early to work out, even when your bed is calling your name. It's staying late to finish a project, even when you'd rather be relaxing. Discipline is what separates those who achieve their goals from those who only dream about them.

In the world of entrepreneurship, discipline manifests in various ways—setting and adhering to a schedule, following through on commitments, managing finances responsibly, and consistently delivering value to customers. It's easy to get caught up in the excitement of new ideas and projects, but without discipline, that excitement can fizzle out before it leads to tangible results.

Kobe Bryant's legendary work ethic is a perfect example of discipline in action. Known for his relentless dedication to his craft, Kobe would arrive at the gym hours before his teammates and stay long after they left. While others were content with good enough, Kobe pushed himself to be the best. His discipline wasn't just about physical training; it extended to his mental game, his study of the sport, and his unwavering commitment to excellence. The rings, the accolades, the legacy—they were all byproducts of his disciplined approach to his craft.

Discipline isn't something you're born with; it's a skill you develop over time. It starts with small habits—waking up at the same time every day, sticking to a daily routine, holding yourself accountable for your actions. As you build discipline in one area of your life, it naturally spills over into others. Before you know it, you're not just dreaming about success—you're actively creating it.

Accountability and Self-Reflection

Discipline is closely tied to accountability. To be successful, you need to hold yourself accountable for your actions, your decisions, and your progress. This means being honest with yourself about where you're falling short, where you need to improve, and where you need to push harder. It's easy to point fingers and blame external factors for our shortcomings, but true growth comes from taking responsibility for our own lives.

Every morning when you look in the mirror, ask yourself: Am I doing everything I can to achieve my goals? Am I making the most of my time, my resources, my talents? Am I being honest with myself about where I'm at and where I need to go? These are tough questions, but they're necessary if you want to succeed.

Self-reflection is a powerful tool in your entrepreneurial arsenal. It allows you to assess your progress, identify areas for improvement, and make necessary adjustments to your strategy. But self-reflection is only effective if you're willing to be brutally honest with yourself. This means acknowledging your mistakes, understanding your weaknesses, and taking proactive steps to overcome them.

Accountability also involves setting clear, measurable goals and tracking your progress toward them. Without goals, you're simply drifting, reacting to whatever life throws your way. With goals, you have a clear direction, a roadmap for where you want to go. And with accountability, you ensure that you stay on course, even when the going gets tough.

Taking the Leap

So, what does all of this mean for you? It means that it's time to stop waiting, stop making excuses, and start taking action. The path to success isn't paved with good intentions; it's built on hard work, discipline, and the willingness to take risks.

You don't need to have everything figured out to begin. You don't need to wait for the perfect conditions. The time to act is now. Yes, there will be challenges. Yes, there will be failures. But every step you take brings you closer to your goal. Every action you take is a vote for the person you want to become.

Remember, the entrepreneurial journey is not a sprint; it's a marathon. It requires endurance, resilience, and a willingness to keep moving forward, no matter what obstacles you encounter. There will be days when you feel like giving up, when the challenges seem insurmountable. But those are the days that matter most. Those are the days when you prove to yourself—and to the world—that you have what it takes to succeed.

Building a Legacy

As you reach the end of this journey through "The Entrepreneur Outline," remember that everything you've learned, every principle you've embraced, every strategy you've planned means nothing without action. The final chapter of your journey isn't written on these pages—it's written in your actions, your decisions, your commitment to move forward, no matter what.

You have the tools, the knowledge, and the potential. The only thing left to do is to act. Don't wait for the right time—create it. Don't wait for the perfect conditions—make them. Don't wait for the opportunities—seize them.

Success is waiting for you, but it won't wait forever. The time to start is now. So go out there and make it happen. Write your own story, build your own legacy, and become the entrepreneur you were always meant to be.

The Entrepreneur's Code

In closing, I want to leave you with what I call "The Entrepreneur's Code"—a set of guiding principles to keep you grounded and focused as you embark on this journey:

1. Take Responsibility: Your life, your success, your future—it's all in your hands. No one else is responsible for your outcomes but you.

2. Embrace Action: Don't wait for the right time. Start now, adjust along the way, and keep moving forward.

3. Pursue Excellence: Always strive to be the best version of yourself. Never settle for mediocrity.

4. Value Time: Time is your most precious asset. Use it wisely, invest it in things that matter, and never take it for granted.

5. Stay Disciplined: Success is built on discipline. Develop the habits that lead to greatness, and stick to them, even when it's hard.

6. Seek Growth: Always be learning, always be improving. The moment you stop growing is the moment you start falling behind.

7. Face Challenges Head-On: Don't shy away from obstacles. Embrace them as opportunities to grow, learn, and become stronger.

8. Build a Legacy: Think beyond the present. What do you want to leave behind? What impact do you want to have on the world? Make decisions that contribute to your legacy.

9. Never Quit: There will be times when you want to give up, when the path seems too difficult. But remember, the only way to fail is to quit. Keep going, no matter what.

10. Believe in Yourself: At the end of the day, the most important factor in your success is your belief in yourself. If you don't believe you can do it, no one else will.

This is your time. Don't wait for the right moment, because the right moment is now. Take what you've learned, apply it, and start building the life you've always dreamed of. The world is waiting for you to make your mark. Go out there and make it happen.

The Entrepreneurial Promise

Promise yourself that from this moment on, you will take full control of your future. Promise that you will stop waiting and start doing. Promise that you will commit to the hard work, the discipline, and the resilience it takes to succeed. And most importantly, promise that you will never, ever give up on your dreams.

The entrepreneur's journey is not for the faint of heart. It's for those who are willing to take risks, to face their fears, and to push beyond their limits. It's for those who refuse to settle for anything less than the best version of themselves. It's for you.

So as you close this book, remember: the journey doesn't end here. It's just beginning. Now is the time to step up, take action, and start building the life you want. Your future is in your hands. Go out there and create it.

BIO

I have been drumming for over two decades now, my life has taught me a lot. From living in Modesto California to now living in Nashville Tennesse. From teaching music to the disabled and watching music literally and physically impact their life. To working for some of the biggest bands in the world on some of the biggest stages in the world. From playing drums with Grammy award winning musicians to playing drums for tv shows. From getting endorsed as a drummer to getting my own signature on my drumsticks. From acting and being in tv shows and watching myself on tv, to acting in award winning movies and watching myself in "sold-out" movie theaters to acting in music videos that have gotten millions of views...

The list just keeps going...

My story is a complexed story. Growing up with a single mother we were raised in a cult. From escaping my childhood finally at 16 years old and everyone around me didn't think I would even finish high school. To starting college and getting hit by a car and laying on what could have been my death bed, to finishing college and really being a light to many other people.

The Entrepreneurial Outline

I stand here today sharing my story with the hopes of if I could help somebody -If I could just add value to one person, how much of an impact could we make?

Made in the USA
Columbia, SC
24 October 2024